THE OWL AND THE PUSSY-CAT

THE OWL AND THE PUSSY-CAT

by Edward Lear
illustrated by Justin Todd

LONDON · VICTOR GOLLANCZ LTD · 1990

Also illustrated by Justin Todd

ALICE'S ADVENTURES IN WONDERLAND

THROUGH THE LOOKING-GLASS
and What Alice Found There

THE WIND IN THE WILLOWS

THE TWELVE DAYS OF CHRISTMAS

First published in Great Britain 1990
by Victor Gollancz Ltd
14 Henrietta Street, London WC2E 8QJ

Illustrations copyright © 1990 by Justin Todd

The right of Justin Todd to be identified as author of
the illustrations has been asserted by him in accordance
with the Copyright, Designs and Patents Act 1988.

British Library Cataloguing in Publication Data
Lear, Edward 1812–1888
The owl and the pussy-cat.
I. Title
821.8

ISBN 0-575-04709-7

Printed in Hong Kong for Imago Publishing Ltd

For Barbara

The Owl and the Pussy-cat
went to sea
In a beautiful pea-green boat,

They took some honey,
　　and plenty of money,
Wrapped up in a five-pound note.

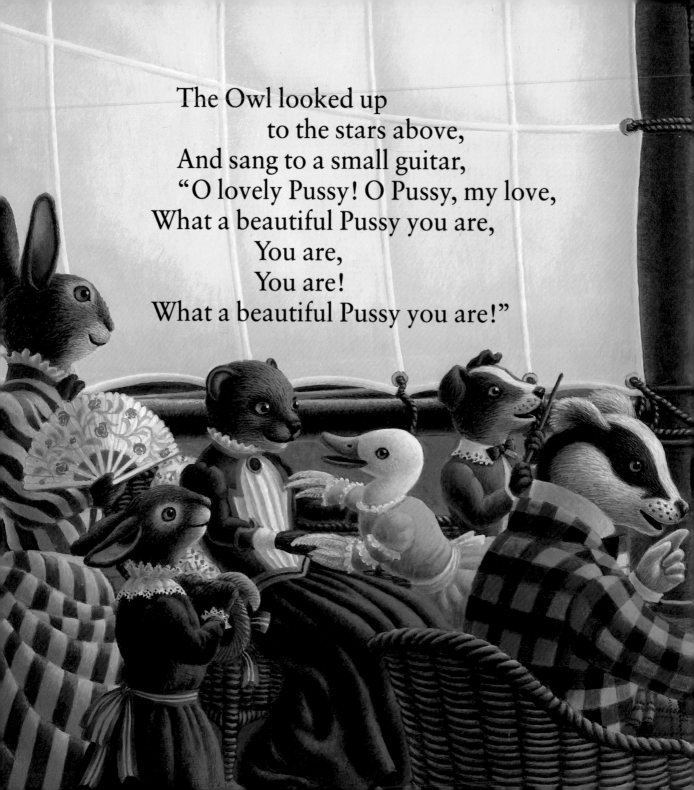

The Owl looked up
to the stars above,
And sang to a small guitar,
"O lovely Pussy! O Pussy, my love,
What a beautiful Pussy you are,
You are,
You are!
What a beautiful Pussy you are!"

Pussy said to the Owl,
        "You elegant fowl!
How charmingly sweet you sing!
O let us be married!
        too long we have tarried:
But what shall we do for
                a ring?"

They sailed away,

for a year

and a day,

To the land
where the Bong-tree grows

And there in a wood
a Piggy-wig stood
With a ring at the end of his nose,
His nose,
His nose,
With a ring at the end of his nose.

"Dear Pig, are you willing
     to sell for one shilling
          Your ring?"
Said the Piggy, "I will."

So they took it away,
and were married next day
By the Turkey who lives
on the hill.

They dined on mince,
    and slices of quince,
Which they ate
    with a runcible spoon;

And hand in hand,
        on the edge of the sand,
They danced by the light of the moon,
        The moon,
        The moon,
They danced by the light of the moon.

THE OWL AND THE PUSSY-CAT

I

The Owl and the Pussy-cat went to sea
  In a beautiful pea-green boat,
They took some honey, and plenty of money,
  Wrapped up in a five-pound note.
The Owl looked up to the stars above,
  And sang to a small guitar,
'O lovely Pussy! O Pussy, my love,
  What a beautiful Pussy you are,
    You are,
    You are!
  What a beautiful Pussy you are!'

II

Pussy said to the Owl, 'You elegant fowl!
  How charmingly sweet you sing!
O let us be married! too long we have tarried:
  But what shall we do for a ring?'
They sailed away, for a year and a day,
  To the land where the Bong-tree grows
And there in a wood a Piggy-wig stood
  With a ring at the end of his nose,
    His nose,
    His nose,
  With a ring at the end of his nose.

III

'Dear Pig, are you willing to sell for one shilling
  Your ring?' Said the Piggy, 'I will.'
So they took it away, and were married next day
  By the Turkey who lives on the hill.
They dined on mince, and slices of quince,
  Which they ate with a runcible spoon;
And hand in hand, on the edge of the sand,
  They danced by the light of the moon,
    The moon,
    The moon,
  They danced by the light of the moon.

BASIC
JEWELLERY
MAKING
TECHNIQUES

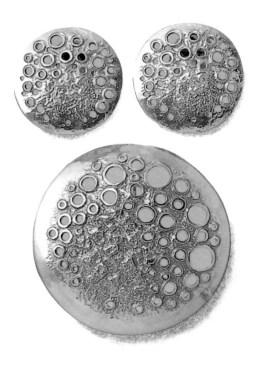

BASIC
JEWELLERY
MAKING
TECHNIQUES

JINKS McGRATH

GREENWICH EDITIONS

A QUANTUM BOOK

This edition published by
Greenwich Editions
10 Blenheim Court
Brewery Road
London N7 9NT

ISBN 0-86288-151-X

QUMJMT

This book was produced by
Quantum Books Ltd
6 Blundell Street
London N7 9BH

Printed in Singapore by Star Standard Industries Pte. Ltd.

Contents

INTRODUCTION 7

1 PLANNING
YOUR WORKSHOP 9

2 DESIGNING
YOUR OWN PROJECTS 23

3 BASIC
TECHNIQUES 29

4 ADVANCED
TECHNIQUES 63

TECHNICAL INFORMATION 108

GLOSSARY 109

INDEX 111

Introduction

For centuries throughout the world jewellery and the means of self-adornment have fascinated both men and women. From the traditional creations of tribal peoples to today's sophisticated products of the well-known jewellery houses of New York, Paris, London and Rome, jewellery has always been used as a public display of wealth and culture as well as, more intimately, an expression of self and of perceived taste.

The creation of jewellery goes far deeper than the desire simply to reveal wealth and to set or follow fashion, however. In most cities of the world, in basements and hidden away in back streets, are the workshops that produce the glittering displays that appear in the windows of fashionable stores. Throughout the world there are hundreds of skilled men and women producing work in conditions and by methods that have changed little over the centuries. For some of these people, their workshop is little more than a block of wood held in sand and a few simple tools, and the skills they use have been unchanged for generations.

Technology has, of course, made its influence felt. Machines now produce lengths of intricate chains; heavy mills and presses extrude sheets of fine metal; complicated electroplating and photo-etching systems produce in minutes what once took hours; and sophisticated casting techniques create high quality finishes. But these mechanized processes have not meant that the hand-worker no longer has a role; they have merely made the world of jewellery a more competitive place.

Traditional methods of producing jewellery continue to thrive, but a more contemporary school has found its niche in the market. Specialist jewellers, who design and make everything themselves, play an important part in the art and craft movement. Many art and design colleges offer degree courses in metalwork, silver-smithing or jewellery making, and adult education

courses covering every aspect of the craft are widely available. Many of those who follow a course will find that they want to go on to make jewellery professionally; others find that they enjoy the challenge jewellery making offers as a hobby; and still others want to pursue it on a part-time basis only, so that they can enjoy the creative aspects without having to rely on it as a means of earning a living. Those who are fortunate enough to keep jewellery making as a hobby can allow themselves to be wholly creative in their approach, following some ideas through to the end and abandoning those that seem not to "work", without the pressures of the marketplace putting constraints on their inventiveness.

Whichever of these groups you fall into, I hope that you will find this book useful. In the first chapters I discuss the equipment you will need to set up a small workshop and explain how best your workshop should be laid out. Five projects are described in detail, the step-by-step processes involved using both the basic and more advanced techniques discussed from page 63. These projects can, of course, be modified to suit your own interpretation of the design, although you will still need to use the same basic techniques.

As you become more familiar with the required techniques and processes, you will be able to develop your own style, which may involve your using some techniques rather than others. Most jewellers who work on their own tend to become highly skilled in one or other area and rarely use other techniques – which brings us back full circle to the traditional workshops and methods of making jewellery.

Enjoy making jewellery in your own workshop – a place where ideas can flourish and your skills develop, and where you can enjoy the satisfaction of creating something personal and beautiful.

How to Use this Book

This book is written as an instructional guide for those people who want to learn about the craft of precious jewellery making. Reference is made to "silver" throughout, being the material I used in all the techniques and step-by-step projects. In most cases, copper, brass or nickel silver could be used in place of silver, but annealing and soldering temperatures do vary a little (see Technical Information). Using gold for jewellery making is wonderful but expensive, so it is advisable to first familiarize yourself with silver before embarking on an ambitious gold project.

The book is divided into six sections. The first deals with the equipment and materials you need to set up a practical workshop. I have listed essential tools you need to get started and also a selection of other tools which can be added to your workshop as you progress. A short section on design will help you find ways of looking for ideas and translating them into pieces of jewellery. This is followed by a section on basic jewellery-making techniques. These are all needed to make the first two "step-by-step" projects, so do read through the techniques and, preferably, work through them before attempting the projects.

The section on more advanced techniques gives you a broad description of each technique and the tools you need, but do read further detailed descriptions if you wish to pursue any of these techniques more seriously. I recommend Oppi Untracht's *Metal Techniques for Craftsmen,* which gives very detailed accounts of almost anything you need to know. For some of the more advanced techniques, quite a lot of specialist equipment is needed, so it is worthwhile experimenting at an evening class before deciding whether or not you want to invest in your own tools.

I have dealt separately with the working properties of gold. These differ from those of silver and special care must be taken when annealing or soldering different carat and coloured golds.

Lastly, some useful tables give annealing and soldering temperatures, formulas for lengths and circumferences, how to estimate costs and comparative weights and measures.

CHAPTER ONE

Planning Your Workshop

The great advantages of making jewellery are that you need only a relatively small space in which to work, it is a tremendously challenging and exciting craft to learn, and you need never again worry about buying gifts for loved ones. The only drawback is that it can be expensive, especially at first when there seems to be an endless list of tools to buy. Don't be put off, however – you can produce a wonderful range of items with just a few basic tools.

Laying Out Your Workshop

It is surprising how little space you will need, and if you plan your workshop carefully it will serve you for many years. There are a few basic dos and don'ts, which are listed below, but in general you should work in an area where you feel comfortable, adding equipment as and when you find you need and can afford individual items.

▌ Try to avoid siting your workshop in an area where bright sunlight will fall directly on your work, especially the soldering area. It is difficult to see colours change as you heat up silver if the light is very bright.

▌ When you are dealing with acids and other chemicals, you must make sure that the room is well ventilated. Whether you are working in a kitchen, bathroom or specially created workroom, there must be a good flow of air.

▌ You will need access to several power points so that there are no extension leads trailing across the floor. You should also avoid having electric flexes lying across your workbench where they may easily be damaged by flames or acid.

▌ Try to have a good artificial light source, which can be easily turned on and off, directly above your work area.

▌ If possible, keep the area in which you polish your work separate, because the dust created by polishing is dirty and will get onto your other work.

▌ Keep a lighter near to your soldering torch. Always remember to turn off the flame when the torch is not in use unless it has a pilot light.

▌ If you are fortunate enough to have a special workroom, you should make sure that there is a stainless steel sink and draining board.

▌ Do not keep tools and equipment made of ferrous metal above or near to acid because the fumes will quickly cause rust.

▌ If your working area is cold in winter, use an electric heater rather than a portable gas one. The condensation caused by gas heaters will quickly make your ferrous tools rust.

It is a good idea to have a notice board in your workshop. Keep a sheet of paper pinned to it, and when you think you are going to need a particular tool, make a note of it. Before you go to the craft shop, list those items and tools that you *really* need, omitting those that you can manage without. In this way you will, over the months and years, build up a stock of carefully selected and versatile tools.

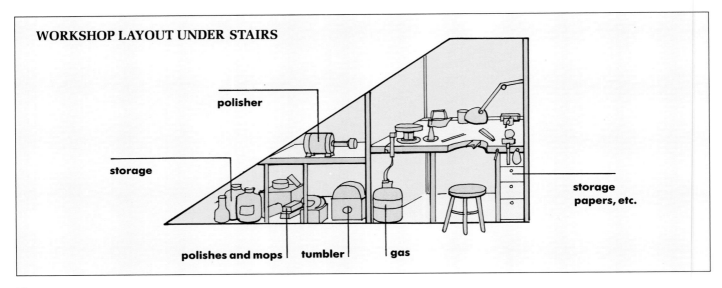

WORKSHOP LAYOUT UNDER STAIRS

polisher

storage

storage papers, etc.

polishes and mops   tumbler   gas

WORKSHOP LAYOUT IN A ROOM

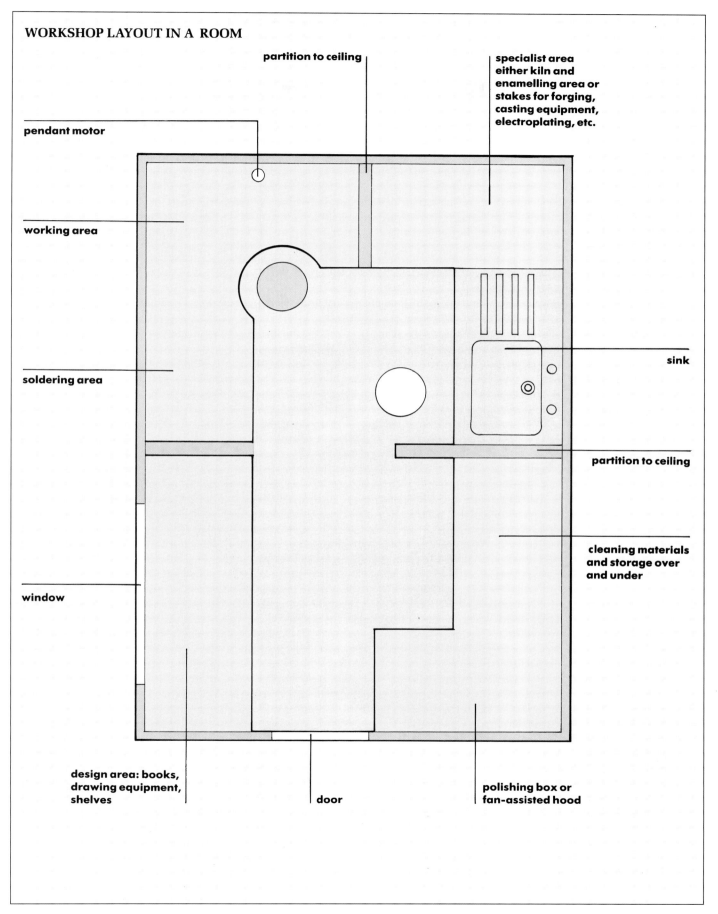

partition to ceiling

specialist area
either kiln and
enamelling area or
stakes for forging,
casting equipment,
electroplating, etc.

pendant motor

working area

soldering area

sink

partition to ceiling

cleaning materials
and storage over
and under

window

design area: books,
drawing equipment,
shelves

door

polishing box or
fan-assisted hood

Essential Tools

Your first requirement is a table or bench on which to work. The kitchen table may do to start with, but I would not recommend it for the long term. The sooner you can find a little corner of your own where you can safely leave your work unattended, the better! An old table will make a suitable bench, but do make sure that it has sturdy legs. The recommended height for all benches is about 90cm which will give support to your elbows while you are sitting in an upright position.

You can make your own workbench by using a sheet of 25mm plywood, 1.8 × 1.2m. Cut a semicircle approximately 60cm across in the centre of one of the long sides. Fix the table top to a firm base, making sure that nothing obstructs the semicircular opening. Fasten a strong piece of calico or leather around the underside of the semicircle, holding it in place with hooks. This will catch all the filings and scrap metal pieces, which can be collected from time to time, taken to the refiners and sold.

A useful and portable workbench. It should be fixed to the floor to give maximum stability.

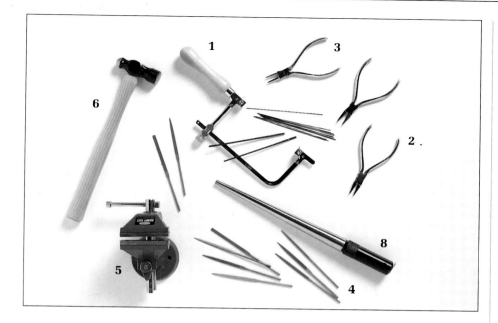

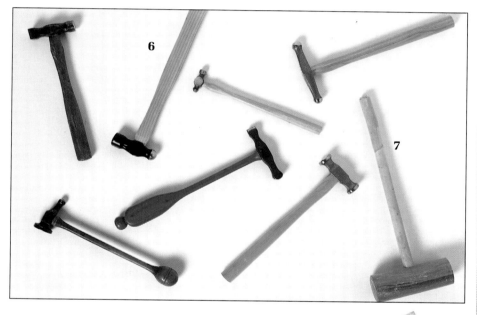

1 Piercing saw and blades You will keep this tool forever. The blades come in packets of 12, and it is cheaper to buy a gross. Start off with blade numbers 2/0, 1/0 and 1.

2 Flat-nose pliers Buy two pairs of pliers, with oval ends or with straight ends. Keep a look out for a very small pair.

3 Round-nose pliers These are useful for bending wire, and you should get a large pair and a small pair.

4 Needle files These are used extensively for refining shapes, removing solder and levelling surfaces, and you will need flat, oval, triangular and semicircular ones. Needle files are available in packets of 8 or 10, and this is a good way to buy them.

5 Small vice There are two different sorts of vice that you will find useful. A jeweller's vice has a ball joint, which means that it can be used in all angles, and "safe" jaws. A small bench vice (see opposite) is sturdier for most jobs, and you can make your own safe jaws from copper or wood if necessary.

6 Hammer A general-purpose hammer is called a ball-pein (or ball-peen) hammer.

7 Wooden mallet Wooden mallets are generally used to shape silver because they do not leave marks.

8 Steel triblet This tool is essential for shaping rings, wires, collets and so on after soldering. It is also sometimes known as a mandrel.

PIN

Whether you are working from the kitchen table or have made your own bench, you will need what is called a "pin". This is a wedge of wood fitted to the centre of the semicircle in the bench or held with a G-clamp to a table. Some jewellers cut a V up the middle of the wedge so that the silver can rest on the wood while the piercing saw works up the V. It also supports the work while it is being filed, cleaned, set, burnished and so on. In other words, it is a vital part of your equipment.

A pin that is suitable to fix to a transportable workbench (below) and an example of a permanent fixture to a bench (above).

Recommended Tools

Listed here are some of the other useful tools that are worth keeping a look out for as you progress with your skills.

KEY:

1 Riffler files
2 Wooden punches
3 Ring sizers
4 Doming block
5 Anvil or flatplate
6 Arkansas stone
7 Large files

8 Drawplates
9 Top cutters/side cutters
10a Half-round pliers
10b Parallel pliers
10c Serrated pliers
11 Crucible
12 Scriber or scribe
13a Drill bits
13b Bow drill

13c Hand vice or drill
14 Metal punches
15 Swage block
16 Burnishers
17 Suede stick and emery sticks
18 Sandbag
19 Hand vice and ring holder
20 Jointing tool

1 Riffler files These curved files allow you to file in corners, on curves and in generally inaccessible places.

2 Wooden punches Punches are used for all sorts of "forming" work. Wooden ones shape without marking, and it is useful to have a range of diameters.

3 Ring sizers These come in sizes A–Z and can be obtained in the form of a sizing card, a ring set of 26 or a set of 52 with ½ sizes.

4 Doming block Usually brass and available in different sizes, the most useful being a 5cm cube. This is used for making domes and semicircles of silver. It should be kept clean and dry. Any bits lying in the bottom of the block will mark the silver. The diameter of the silver should be slightly less than that of the dome hole.

5 Anvil or flatplate Either of these tools is useful when you are flattening or hammering silver. The size does not really matter, but the surface should be kept smooth, clean and dry.

6 Arkansas stone You will need to keep your gravers, scorpers and tips sharp. Keep the stone well oiled when you are using it so that loose particles do not become embedded in the tool being sharpened.

7 Large files You will need oval, flat and half-round files.

8 Drawplates These steel plates have graded holes, which are used to reduce the diameter or outline of round or sectional wire and tube.

9 Top cutters/side cutters These are useful for cutting up small paillons of solder, for cutting wire and for getting into small difficult places.

10 Pliers You will eventually find that you will need several types of pliers. *Half-round pliers* can be used to bend metal into curves without marking the outside. *Parallel pliers* will grip a piece of silver equally along its length. *Snipe pliers* can be used in the same way as flat-nose pliers, but they can reach into difficult places. *Serrated pliers* are useful for gripping ends of wire when you need to pull it through the drawplate or straighten it in a vice. The serrations will mark the silver.

11 Crucible You will need a crucible to melt scrap and pour it into an ingot mould.

12 Scriber or scribe This little tool is used for marking a pattern on the silver and for marking lines, and circle centres. It should be kept clean and with a good point.

13 Drills Use an ordinary *hand drill* to make large holes. When you need to make small holes, use a *bow drill,* which allows you to hold your work with one hand while the drill is operated with the other. Wind the string around the shaft by twisting the top, and then, with the wooden handle held securely between two fingers, push the drill down. Allow it to rise, which it will do because of the tension on the string, then push it down again. You can make fine *drill bits* from sewing needles, which are broken in half. Rub two opposite faces flat on your arkansas stone (soapstone), and then rub off the other two corners. Small *hand vices* or *drills,*

which can be used with one hand, are available with different-sized chucks, which will take drills from 2mm to 0.5mm.

14 Metal punches Used in conjunction with the doming block, metal punches have all of the uses of wooden punches, but are harder and more precise.

15 Swage block This can be used with the handles of your metal punch to shape a strip of silver into a U shape. The silver should be slightly narrower than the slot into which it is being punched.

16 Burnisher Burnishers are used for rubbing and polishing your finished work. They are also used for setting stones, by rubbing the silver over the stone. They should be kept dry and polished.

17 Suede stick and emery stick Both are used for cleaning and finishing. The emery stick should be used first, and it is possible to dissolve polish onto a suede stick with lighter fuel.

18 Sandbag This provides a good supportive base for silver when it is being shaped with either wooden or metal punches, or as a support when engraving.

19 Ring holder and hand vice A ring holder can be adjusted by means of a wedge to accommodate a ring of any size, and it will also support your work while you are working. The shank of a ring can be held in the protected jaws of the hand vice while you work on a setting.

20 Jointing tool This tool is used to hold chenier and wire straight while it is cut with a piercing saw.

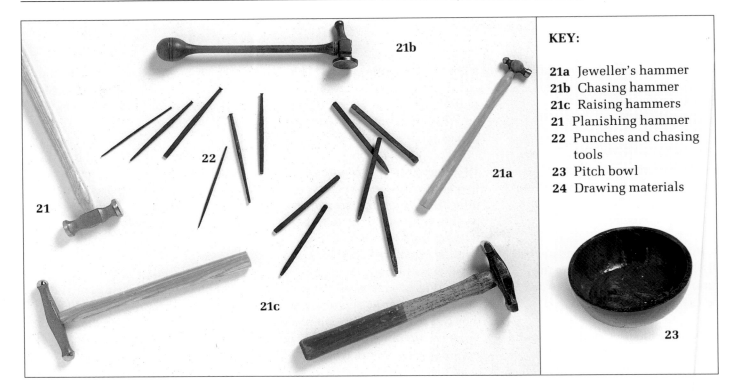

KEY:

21a Jeweller's hammer
21b Chasing hammer
21c Raising hammers
21 Planishing hammer
22 Punches and chasing tools
23 Pitch bowl
24 Drawing materials

21 Hammers A selection of hammers will be useful. A *jeweller's hammer* can be used to tap soft and thin silver. A *chasing hammer* should be used to strike the heads of repoussé and chasing tools. This type of hammer has a broad head and a rounded handle so that you can deliver rhythmic strokes. A *raising hammer* has a round nose, which is used to compress silver, while the flat face is used to extend the metal. Gentle taps with a *planishing hammer* will allow you to remove marks made by your raising or ball-pien hammer.

22 Punches and chasing tools These are used for shaping and marking silver. They can be bought in sets, or you can make them from square or round steel stock, tempered and ground or filed to shape. Keep your punches clean and dry.

23 Pitch bowl Pitch is used to hold your work firm when you are shaping, engraving, setting stones, chasing and doing repoussé work.

It is made from a mixture of asphaltum, plaster of Paris or pumice powder and tallow or linseed oil. To make a stiffer pitch, add more plaster of Paris; to keep it soft, add more tallow or linseed. Pitch can be removed by being burnt, when it forms ash, or by being dissolved in turpentine. The bowl sits in a round wooden ring to keep it steady in all angles.

24 Drawing materials Set aside an area of your workroom for drawing materials and equipment. Keep a good supply of sharp pencils, tracing paper, drawing pads and rubbers, and you will also find dividers, compasses, a steel rule, a calculator, templates of circles, curves, rectangles and squares, a micrometer, steel square and a craft knife invaluable.

A pair of dividers and a steel rule graduated in inches and centimetres are invaluable to your work.

Soldering Equipment

A wide variety of different pieces of equipment is available for producing the heat needed during the manufacture of jewellery. Listed here are just a few of the torches and their gas supplies.

You will need to set aside an area on your workbench for soldering. If you are right handed, try the area to your left, because you will find it more convenient and practical to have your files, drills, vices and so on your right. If you are left handed, do the opposite. Alternatively, find a completely separate area for your soldering – one in which flames and acids will not threaten your other tools. If you do solder on the bench, make sure that the torch is readily to hand and insert a hook to hang it on. To guard against accidental burning, protect your soldering area with a heat-resistant mat, an old oven tin or a revolving soldering stand. You will also need a charcoal block or synthetic soldering block. A charcoal block helps the work heat up quickly but will burn through quickly if it is left to smoulder. A soldering block is particularly useful when large work is heated because it does not burn through. However, soldering takes a little longer as the block does not reflect the heat.

Keep a good supply of paint brushes, old toothbrushes, empty jam jars and an assortment of heat-resistant dishes handy in your workshop. They are always useful for cleaning, pickling, applying borax and many other things! Keep a lighter close to your soldering torch.

After heating silver, it is usual to "quench" it. For this you need a 10:1 solution of water and sulphuric acid. This can be purchased ready mixed in the form of safety pickle, or you can buy neat sulphuric acid and prepare your own solution.

Use a glass measuring jug so that you can gauge the correct amount of acid. Wear good quality rubber gloves and a heavy apron or overall.

1   Portable blow torch – too small for general use, but its small direct flame is useful when soldering small chains, wire rings, etc.

2   Adjustable blow torch – the gas supply can come either from the mains or a Propane gas cylinder. The air is introduced by blowing down a flexible rubber pipe fixed onto the torch at point "a". It is a very good multi-purpose torch but not suitable for very large pieces or prolonged high temperatures.

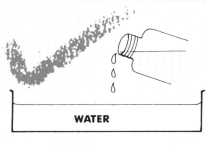

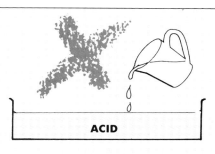

CAUTION
All acids are dangerous and must be handled and stored carefully. When making up your "pickle", add acid to water; never add water to acid.

WATER

Add acid to water

ACID

Never add water to acid

Large Equipment

All the items of equipment listed here are expensive, and it may take you several years to acquire them all. Only consider purchasing these items when they are absolutely necessary, because some of the work they do can be done very satisfactorily by hand. However, I have listed them all to give you some idea of their uses and desirability.

1 Ultrasonic cleaner A stainless steel container is used with an ammonia-based detergent to remove, ultrasonically, excess polish from silver, gold, copper or brass. The work is placed in a rack or on a hook so that it is suspended in the cleaning fluid, through

which the sound waves penetrate. Although this is a very efficient cleaning method, patience, hot water, a toothbrush and detergent will do just as well.

2 Polisher This is basically an electric motor with arms, to which can be attached a variety of mops, brushes and polishes. It can be made from an adapted washing-machine motor, but a minimum of 1800 rpm is necessary for good results. A polisher is essential if you want a highly polished finish. Some are shown below: (2a) Rouge, (2b) Hyfin and (2c) Tripoli. The strings (2e) are used for hand polishing.

3 Rolling mill Rolling mills come in a variety of sizes – and prices. Choose the best one you can afford. They are used for reducing the thickness of silver and of sectional and round wire. If you order materials to your precise requirements, you will not need a mill. Use only silver, copper, gold or brass in your mill: steel will leave dents and pits on the rollers, which will have to be removed professionally.

2d

2e

3

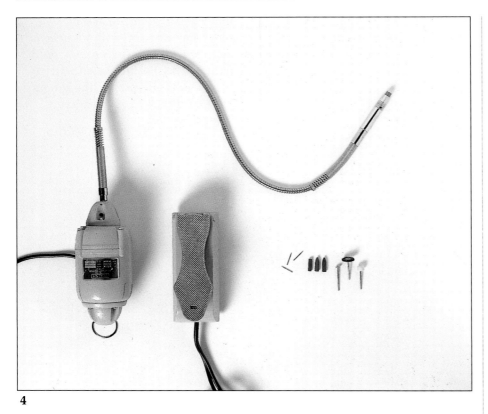

4

4 Pendant motor with flexible shaft This can be very useful. A variety of heads allows you to texture surfaces, to remove solder, to clean inside rings and castings, to polish small areas and to open out settings.

5

6

5 Scales All sorts of scales are available, ranging from hand-held ones to electronic ones. As long as they are accurate for very small weights they will be suitable. You might be fortunate and acquire a set being replaced by a local school or college.

6 Kiln Kilns, which are either gas-fired or electric, are used for enamelling, annealing and casting. The same kiln should not be used for both enamelling and casting, because the burnt-out residues from casting would contaminate the enamel, but annealing may be done in either.

7

8

7 Tumbler/polisher This useful piece of equipment is used for finishing fine work such as chains or rings. It is not suitable for large, flat areas. It consists of a rubber barrel about one-third full of small stainless steel shapes which, when water and special soap flakes are added, burnish the silver. The barrel is turned by a motor, which turns two spindles, and it can be left turning for several hours.

8 Stakes A variety of stakes can be used for shaping and raising larger pieces of silver if you are making spoons, bowls or plates. They should be kept well polished and dry. These are necessary only if you want to concentrate on silver-smithing.

Chemicals

Listed here are some of the acids, cleaning and polishing materials and other items that you will need. All acids and chemicals **must** be stored in a safe, dry and cool place. If children are likely to have access to your work area, you should install a cupboard that can be locked. When you are handling acids and chemicals, **always** work in a well-ventilated area and **always** wear protective clothing.

ACIDS

Nitric acid (HNO_3) is used for etching and, as a "bright dip", for removing fire stain. Use a solution of 3 parts water to 1 part acid. When you etch work, immerse the piece in the acid solution and tickle it with a feather from time to time to ensure that the etch is uniform. Always keep an eye on your work so that it does not etch too quickly. To use nitric acid as a dip to remove fire stain, hang your work by a length of stainless steel wire for a couple of seconds in the solution. The cupric oxides will turn black or grey. Remove the work from the acid solution, rinse it under running water and clean off the black with pumice powder and water. Repeat the process until all the oxides have gone. The acid will begin to attack the solder and silver, so you must immerse your work for only short periods.

Sulphuric acid (H_2SO_4) is used for pickling – that is, for removing oxides after heating – for removing burnt-on flux and for removing grease. Use it in a solution of 10 parts water to 1 part acid.

ACETONE

This colourless, volatile and highly flammable liquid is excellent for cleaning off grease and dirt, but it will leave a mark. It also dissolves many glues, so be careful where you use it. Always store it in a tightly closed container and use it only in a well-ventilated room.

SODA CRYSTALS

Approximately one spoonful of crystals in 0.5l of boiling water will neutralize any residue of acid on your work after pickling. Soldering is impossible if there is any acid present, so it is often necessary to boil your work to remove all traces of acid. Rinse your work thoroughly in cold water.

ARGOTEC

This powder can be mixed with methylated spirits or water to form a paste that can be painted onto your work before soldering to help prevent fire stain.

POTASSIUM SULPHIDE

This is used to oxidize particular areas of work. Use one 12mm cube of potassium sulphide in 0.5l of hot water. (See Finishing on page 42.)

PUMICE POWDER

Keep a container of pumice powder and a toothbrush next to the sink. After soldering and pickling, a quick scrub with pumice and water will help to clean your work. Pumice is abrasive, so do not use it on polished work unless you want a matt finish.

STEEL WOOL

Rub steel wool gently over your finished work to give an interesting matt finish.

LIGHTER FUEL

Apply lighter fuel to a chamois leather, duster, polishing stick or polishing strings before you rub polish on. Hold the leather, duster or strings in a vice, and pull tight before you begin to rub.

JEWELLER'S WAX

This can be used to hold your work while you set stones or engrave it. The wax can be melted onto a flat piece of wood and held in a vice.

WET AND DRY PAPERS

Keep a selection of sandpapers from numbers 220 to 1200.

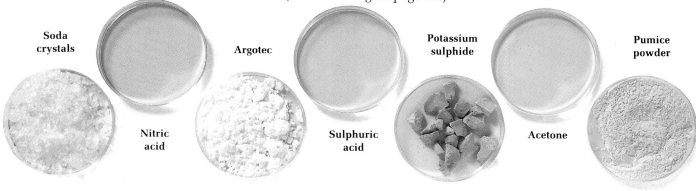

Soda crystals

Argotec

Potassium sulphide

Pumice powder

Nitric acid

Sulphuric acid

Acetone

How to Buy

Silver and gold in sheet form, coils of wire and casting grains.

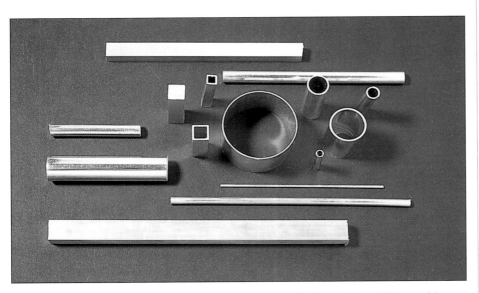

Silver tube and rod of varying sizes and wall thicknesses. The large tube could be used for a napkin ring, thereby eliminating the need for soldering, and the smaller sections have many uses, including stone setting and making hinge joints.

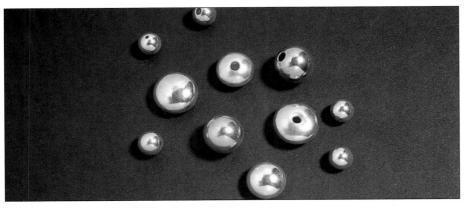

Gold and silver beads with holes already drilled.

METALS

Silver and gold are available in various forms – sheet (which is measured in millimetres or gauges), tube, sectional wire and tube, and rod.

For general-purpose work, standard silver is used. The silver content of Standard or Sterling silver is 92.5 per cent, the remaining 7.5 per cent being copper or other metals. For large pieces, such as bowls and candle-sticks, Brittania silver is often used. This has a silver content of 95.8 per cent. Pure silver or fine silver is very soft and is used mainly during enamelling.

Before you order, work out the exact measurements of the silver you will need. Silver is sold by weight, the price of which varies daily. Collect all the scrap from the calico or leather bag under the pin on your workbench and take it to your bullion dealer once a year. Some jewellers take their annual holidays on the proceeds!

TOOLS

It is possible to find a number of good tools in second-hand tool stores. Before you buy there are a few things to look out for. Check the tips of pairs of pliers to make sure that they close together correctly. Make sure that they are not badly marked, because any dents will transfer to the silver. Look out for badly marked hammers, stakes and punches. Although they can be reground or polished, it may not be worth it. Remember that most second-hand files have been used for iron, steel or aluminium, and I would not recommend them for jewellery making. Second-hand vices, anvils, hand drills and pendant motors, however, are all worth obtaining.

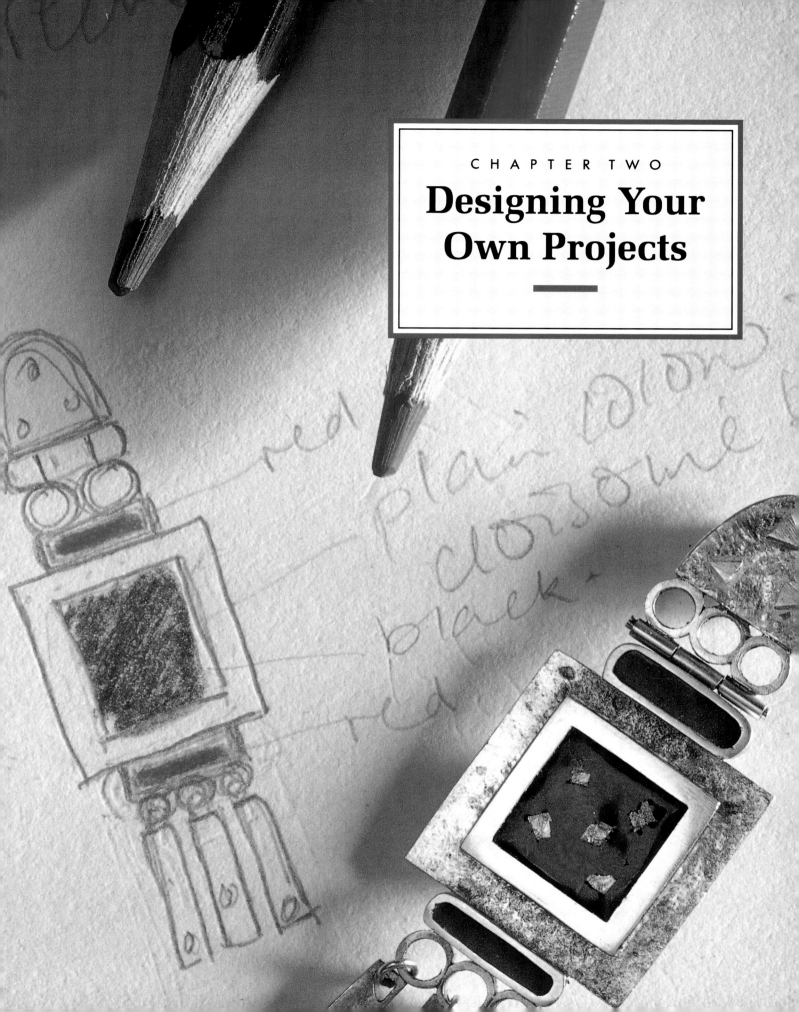

CHAPTER TWO

Designing Your Own Projects

One definition of design is "to form a plan of, to contrive, to purpose, to draw, outline, to sketch a pattern, an intention, scheme, plot . . ." It follows, therefore, that if we design something, the outcome or result is the intention of that design. Finding the inspirational source for a design and translating it into a piece of jewellery that is comfortable to wear, stays in place and does not deteriorate is a very personal process, but in this chapter I shall suggest a few ways of finding the sources and some practical ways of making them work.

These black and white photographs show the wonderful lines and textures that can be found on a beach (*above left*), and a creeping ivy (*above right*). A black and white photograph is extremely effective when looking for strong shapes, textures, shadows, etc. Dramatic lines of an old yew forest (*right*).

From the time we get up in the morning until we fall asleep at night we are surrounded by a vast array of nature's gifts and manmade articles, some of which are beautiful, some of which are not. All of them, however, can be drawn upon in our search for inspiration. Even our dreams – if we remember them – can provide a visual quality, translatable into ideas for jewellery. Looking, seeing and touching are the easy part of the design process; the hardest part is translating what inspires us into something we want to make.

We take for granted most of the objects with which we come into contact during the day. Something may cause us to draw breath with pleasure; other items will provoke feelings of exasperation, anger or mere indifference. If you train yourself to be aware of what you take for granted every day – the road you travel to work on, the paper you read in the morning, the exterior walls of the house you live in, the car you drive, even the arrangement of foodstuffs on the supermarket shelf – you will look at them afresh and with more observant eyes, finding the qualities hidden in them all. It may be that their relationship to the space around them is more interesting than the objects themselves. What isn't there is often just as fascinating as what is.

What else do you take for granted? What about a tree you see every day? Whether it is in the city or the country, it is forever changing. Do you see all the changes or notice them only when the tree is bare? If you really make an effort to take note of objects you do not usually notice, you will find yourself seeing all sorts of shapes and patterns that were just waiting to be seen.

It is always useful to have a more direct source of inspiration, and few things are better or more

VIEW THROUGH A BEECH FOREST

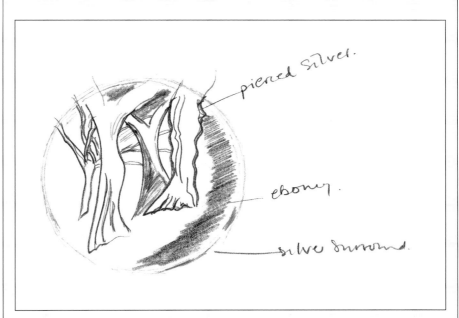

I used a black and white photograph taken in a beech forest and traced roughly over the outline and then refined the drawing. I used silver for the trees in the foreground and an African Blackwood background – a role reversal.

GOLD AND EMERALD NECKLACE

This photograph taken on the hills shows tree lines and hedgerows.

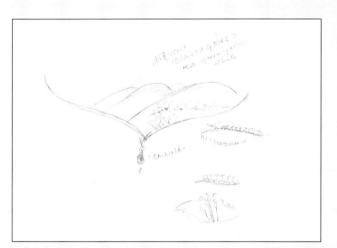

I sketched an idea for a neckpiece using the line of the hills.

The red, white, yellow and green golds used in this piece portray the colours of the hills and the emerald emphasises the green of the country.

SILVER AND WOOD NECKLACE

This photograph shows a local landmark which has suffered the effects of high winds.

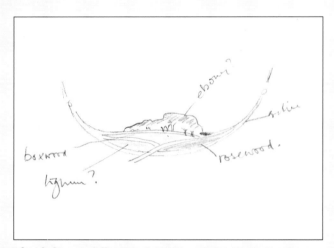

I decided to use different coloured woods to give credence to the subject of the piece.

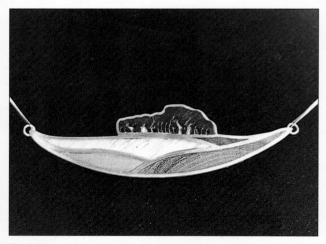

The fields are Rosewood, Boxwood, Acacia and *Lignum Vitae*. The coppice is African Blackwood and is inlaid into silver.

rewarding than a visit to a favourite museum or even to a specific area of a museum. Look out for interesting exhibitions that are being put on in your area; keep a watch for changing shows at galleries; visit your local library and spend time leafing through illustrated books with good photographs. Do not look only at books on jewellery – art, porcelain and china, furniture, glass and all the other creative media can be used as the basis of your designs. Make a note of items you really appreciate and try to understand what it is you like about them. Think about the artists and craftspeople whose work influences you most. Decide what shapes and textures appeal to you. Do you like romantic images or clear-cut, crisp images? Are you nostalgic or do you prefer what might come tomorrow? Once you are confident that you understand your own preferences and dislikes, you will begin to feel confident in your own design ideas.

If you keep a little sketch pad with you, you can make a quick sketch or write a few notes whenever you see something exciting. You do not have to be brilliant at drawing – all you need do is to make a sketch or write a few words to remind yourself of the image. If you prefer, take a camera with you everywhere – black and white film is better than colour for revealing clarity of shape and texture – and whenever you see an interesting outline, reflection or shadow, photograph it. Buy post-cards from museums and galleries you have visited and cut out illustrations from magazines and pin them up in your workshop. Collect interesting stones, buds or leaves, and find space in your workshop for them, so that they are easy to see and pick up. If you are happy with all the things surrounding you, you will give

The pieces on this page by Ruta Brown suggest the textures of the fungus (*above*), and the colour combination of the stones inspires an autumnal feeling.

your designs a good start.

As soon as you have identified your sources of inspiration, you can start to sketch roughly those that appeal to you most. Do not be disappointed if what you believed was a great idea just does not lead anywhere. Forget it and go on to something new, which may well take you in a completely different direction, which may even bring

you back to the original idea with all the difficulties solved.

Once you have made a rough sketch of your idea, try to see it three-dimensionally. Work out where the fittings will go, how it will balance, what materials, including the stones, you will use, then work out the order of making it. Try to decide how it will fit together, and what soldering

should be done first, and what can be left till last. As long as you can see your idea clearly in your mind's eye, a detailed drawing is not really necessary. Obviously, if you need to pierce an exact shape, you will need to make a careful drawing, but with practice the sketches and drawings become easier to prepare.

Designing is the most stimulating part of your jewellery making. Seeing your ideas emerging into a tangible piece of jewellery is tremendously exciting. You will

Pages from a sketch book (*above*) show how ideas for an engagement ring are developed around an oval labradorite and round aquamarine.

The finished ring (*below*) with interlocking wedding ring set with a ruby.

find the ideas flowing over into each other, so do not be afraid to drop bad ones. Some days it all comes easily; other days you will find yourself staring at a blank sheet of paper, wondering where all your ideas have gone. That is the time to take yourself out for a walk in the country, to visit a museum or to spend a day looking through books. Whatever you do, relax – the ideas will come back, unexpectedly sometimes, so keep a pencil and paper by your bedside, just in case.

CHAPTER THREE

Basic Techniques

Transferring Your Design

When you transfer your design try to use the silver as economically as possible. For example, if your design has a straight edge, use the straight edge of the silver; if you are cutting out more than one piece, do not leave a large space between them, but try to fit them close together.

There are several ways in which you can transfer your design to the silver. Try them all until you find the one that suits you best. Of course, if the pattern or design is very simple, you can draw or scribe it directly onto the silver.

YOU WILL NEED

Silver
Plasticine or eraser
Tracing paper
Sheet of acetate or carbon paper
Soft pencil
Scriber
Masking tape
Adhesive – either spray glue or a glue stick

USING ACETATE

Rub over the surface of the silver with a piece of plasticine or an eraser. Lay a piece of acetate over your design and use a scribe to trace the pattern onto the acetate. Rub soft pencil into the scribed lines, then lay the acetate, scribed side down, on the silver, securing it in place with masking tape. Use the blunt end of the pencil to rub over the acetate so that the lines are transferred to the silver.

Remember that your design will appear in reverse if you do this. This may not matter with some designs – a symmetrical pattern will look the same whichever way round it is traced – or you could turn the silver over after piercing. However, if you prefer, you can transfer your pattern to tracing paper and turn that over before tracing the pattern onto the acetate.

USING CARBON PAPER

Rub over the surface of the silver with a piece of plasticine or an eraser. Transfer your design to tracing paper and attach a piece of carbon paper to the silver, holding it in place with masking tape. Secure the tracing paper in place over the carbon paper and draw over the design, using a fine, hard point. Remove the tracing paper and the carbon. Use a scriber to go over the lines of your design, making sure that you do not accidentally smudge or wipe off the carbon lines as you work. When you have scribed over the whole design, wipe away any carbon marks that remain.

USING TRACING PAPER

Transfer your design to a piece of tracing paper. Cover the back of the tracing paper with spray adhesive or adhesive from a glue stick and leave it to dry for a few seconds. Place the tracing paper over the silver and press it firmly into position. Make sure that the paper is securely attached to the silver, then pierce or cut out your design. Peel away the remains of the tracing paper from the silver when you have finished. Any remaining paper can be removed with cotton wool soaked in acetate.

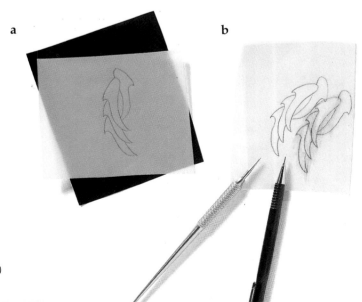

a   b   c

The design is: a) traced through carbon; b) traced through accetate; and c) tracing paper glued onto the silver before piercing.

Sawing and Piercing

When you cut out silver with a piercing saw, the blade will cut only on the down stroke. You should try to develop an easy, rhythmic action and never force the blade. When the blade gets stuck, lift up your work and let the saw find its natural position. You will then be able to continue.

Saw blades are available in sizes 4/0 (finest) up to 14. For most jewellery purposes numbers 4/0 to 4 will give a sufficient range, and number 1/0 is probably a good one to start with. Blades do break easily, so don't think it's just you! They are usually available in packs of 12.

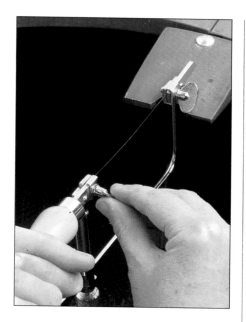

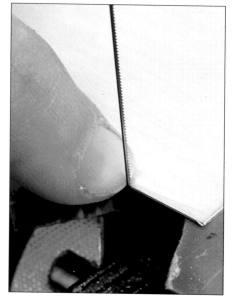

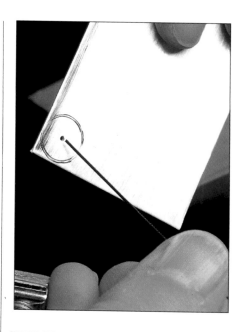

FITTING A BLADE
Take a number 1 blade, with the teeth of the blade towards you and pointing downwards, and slot the top end of the blade into the top fastening of your saw. Tighten the screw. Push the top end of the saw against the bench and slot the bottom end of the blade into the lower fastening of the saw. Tighten the screw. The blade should be firm and springy, with the teeth pointing down towards the handle.

CUTTING
Hold the saw at an angle of 90° to your work. Make the first cut, just touching the blade against your index finger as a guide. Let the blade fall through the silver and continue with a steady up-and-down movement along the line of your pattern.

PIERCING AN ENCLOSED AREA
Drill a small hole in the piece you want to remove. Undo the bottom end of the saw and pass the blade through the hole. Fasten the blade in position again, making sure it is firm, and cut around the enclosed area.

YOU WILL NEED
Piercing saw
3 packets of blades, numbers 1/0
Silver
Small hand drill with a 0.75mm bit

TURNING A CORNER
When you reach a corner, rub the smooth, back edge of the blade into the corner you wish to turn, gradually turning the saw frame until it is facing in the new direction. Do not try to move forwards until the blade is in the correct position.

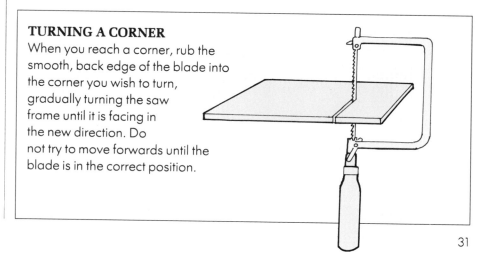

Annealing, Soldering and Pickling

Silver needs to be annealed so that it is not too hard to work easily. When you start work on a new piece of silver, it is wise to anneal it after piercing to make sure it is soft before you start work. Silver needs re-annealing when it becomes work hardened, because if it is too hard it becomes brittle and is liable to crack.

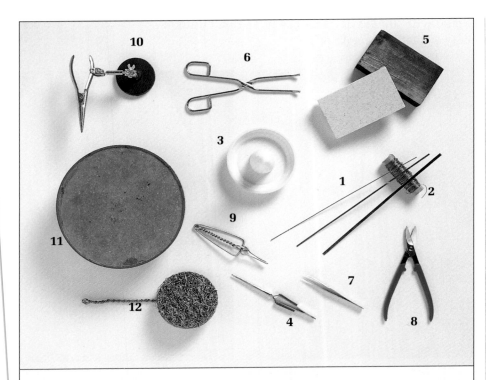

KEY:

1 Hard, medium and easy solders
2 Binding wire
3 Flux or borax
4 Insulated tweezers
5 Charcoal block or soldering block

6 Brass tongs
7 Stainless steel tweezers
8 Snips
9 Springtweezers
10 Third hand
11 Revolving soldering tray
12 Jeweller's wig

YOU WILL NEED

Hard, medium and easy solders
Binding wire
Flux or borax
Insulated tweezers
Charcoal block or soldering block
Gas supply and torch
Pickle
Water
Brass tongs or tweezers
Paintbrush

ANNEALING

Make sure that the area in which you will be working is not in direct light. Put your silver on the soldering block and heat it with a soft flame – that is, in the pale blue area just behind the yellow tip. Feather the flame forwards and back over the silver until it becomes a dull red. Keep the silver that colour for a few seconds, then put out the flame. Quench the silver in the pickle, rinse in water and dry.

SOLDERING

A flame with no added air.

A flame with added air, good for soldering.

A small, hard flame, good for soldering very small areas.

SOLDERING

Soldering is the process of permanently joining one piece of silver to another with heat, flux and solder. It is often necessary to solder more than once on a piece of work, and there are several grades of solder available for doing this.

▌ Enamelling solder has the highest melting point; it is used only if the piece is to be enamelled.

▌ Hard solder is generally the first solder to be used, and it is sometimes used three or four times on the same piece.

▌ Medium solder is used after hard solder. It does not always flow as easily, so cut it into small paillons.

▌ Easy solder is used after medium or hard. It is a good, flowing solder, which is often used for findings.

▌ Extra easy solder is very useful for low-temperature soldering.

Keep a divided dish near the soldering area for strips and paillons of hard, medium and easy solder.

For practical purposes, only hard, medium and easy solders are used for the projects described in this book.

Solder needs a catalyst or agent to make it flow. This is called flux or borax and there are several different types of flux, some being more suitable for high-temperature soldering than others (see Gold, page 93). For most silver work, a borax cone in a dish or a liquid Auflux is suitable.

After fluxing the join apply the solder to your work. Apply the solder in small pieces called paillons. Cut two or three strips up the end of the solder using snips, and then cut across the solder to make small pieces. When you need thinner paillons, roll or hammer the ends of the solder first. Place the paillons in the borax dish so that they are coated in flux. Use the tip of a paintbrush to pick up the paillons and place them around the join or at the bottom of the join for a ring because the solder will flow upwards. Keep any spare paillons in separate small containers, marked "hard", "medium" or "easy".

Heat the work gently with a soft flame. As the water evaporates, the flux will start to bubble, but as soon as all the water has gone, it will settle down. Push any displaced solder back into position with your tweezers. Continue passing the flame over the work until it is heated and has turned a cherry red. At about this point the solder will flow, and a bright, shiny line will appear around the join. Turn off the flame. Quench your work in the pickle, using brass tweezers to place it in and remove it from the acid. Rinse in cold water and dry.

If your work has other joins, you will need to use different solders. Use the same method as before, but replacing the hard solder by medium, and then the medium solder by easy.

TO APPLY THE BORAX

Put a little water in the borax dish and rub the cone in a circular motion to produce a thickish paste. Use a fine paintbrush to apply the borax between the join to be soldered.

BINDING WIRE

When a join needs a little help to stay together during soldering, fasten binding wire around the work and tighten it by twisting the two ends with a pair of flat-nose pliers.

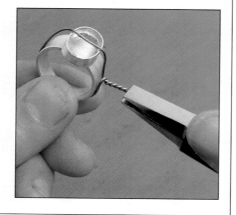

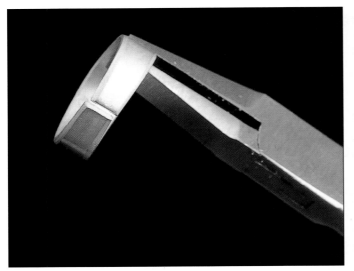

This join is not correctly aligned for soldering. Even if the solder did run, the join would need so much filing down that it would become very thin.

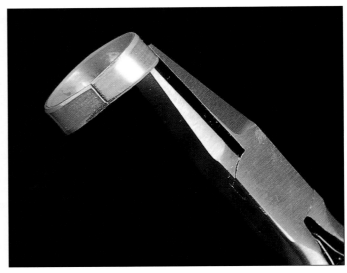

This join is correctly aligned which will, therefore, allow the solder to flow easily.

Solder will *not* run:
▌ If the join is not properly aligned and the gap is too large for the solder to jump
▌ If the join is dirty, or if, after a previous attempt at soldering, there are traces of borax

▌ If there is acid left in the join
▌ If the work is not hot enough
▌ If the flame is too small for the amount of silver to be heated.

You can deliberately stop solder flowing on a previously soldered area by painting the join with a paste of rouge powder and water. However, if you allow the rouge paste to run into the area you want to solder, it won't, so allow the rouged area to dry before fluxing the new join.

On a large join which needs plenty of solder, you may find that a soldering stick is the best method.

Apply flux or borax in the usual way. Cut a long strip of solder and paint it with flux. Hold the solder in insulated soldering tweezers, then heat the work until it is cherry red. When the correct temperature is reached, feed the length of solder into the join, following the line just behind the flame. You can check that the temperature is correct by placing a paillon of the same solder you are using on the outside of the join. As you see it flow, apply the solder stick.

Solder is applied to a join using a soldering stick. Note how the paillon is in place to indicate flowing temperature.

When you need to solder a small piece to a large piece, apply flux and place the solder on the larger piece of work. Hold the smaller piece in soldering tweezers and paint a little flux on the bottom. Add a piece of the same solder and heat the small piece until the solder flows. Heat the large piece until the solder starts to run and use the tweezers to place the small piece on the work, continuing to heat as you work. Remove the flame, holding the piece steady. Quench, rinse and dry your work. Alternatively, paint flux onto both surfaces to be soldered. Place a small piece onto the large piece and place paillons around the join. Gently heat the work from underneath or away from the small piece and, as the solder is about to run, bring the heat onto the small piece. Quench, rinse and dry.

When soldering a small piece to a large piece, first heat the large area before allowing the solder to run.

It is sometimes necessary to alter the position of a finding or to remove a piece that has been soldered. To do this, attach the piece to the charcoal block with binding wire or hold it securely with tweezers. Apply flux to the join you wish to undo and heat the work. As soon as the solder flows, lift up or reposition your work, using the soldering tweezers.

A finding is removed by unsoldering it from the silver sheet.

HOLDING

From time to time you will find it useful to have a "third hand" to help hold pieces while you are soldering. These tools are:
- Insulated soldering tweezers
- Wire tweezers
- Cotter pins
- Jeweller's wig
- Table with adjustable spring pliers.

PICKLING

While it is being heated silver oxidizes and becomes black. When it is placed, still hot, in safety pickle or sulphuric solution, the oxides will disappear. If it is left for a few minutes, flux residues will disappear.

Take care when you are placing hot silver into an acid solution. The acid will spit and give off fumes, so make sure you are working in a well-ventilated area. Unfortunately, the spitting will inevitably cause holes in your clothes, so you should wear a heavy cotton or leather apron at all times in the workshop.

Pickling can be done the other way round. After soldering, quench the piece in water and then drop into a warm solution of sulphuric acid, and hold it at that temperature. This will clean the piece quite rapidly and bring the fine silver to the surface of the work. If it is not practical to pickle in warm acid, you can leave your work overnight in the acid. This will have similar results and is quite safe.

If any acid remains in your work after quenching and pickling, rinse it in water and boil the piece in a solution of hot water and a spoonful of soda crystals. Rinse and dry.

A hot silver piece is placed into the sulphuric acid. Note how the oxides have disappeared from the section that is immersed in the acid solution.

CAUTION

Remove any binding wire before immersing your work in the acid. The metal will contaminate the acid and turn everything pink. If that happens dispose of the acid – it is not possible to clean it. Remember: use only brass tweezers in acid.

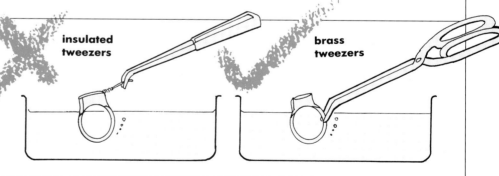

insulated tweezers

brass tweezers

REMOVING FIRE STAIN

Because standard silver contains 7.5 per cent copper, when it is heated in air the copper on the surface oxidizes and leave a black mark on the polished silver. This can be removed in a variety of ways:
- File it off, taking care not to lose the shape of the work
- Rub a dampened "water of Ayr" stone over the mark to form a greyish paste. Keep rinsing off the paste to check that the stain has disappeared
- Before soldering, coat your work with Argotec mixed with water or methylated spirits. Avoid painting this mixture into any solder joins because Argotec is basically a flux and would cause the solder to run. Pickle off after use
- Have your work silver plated.

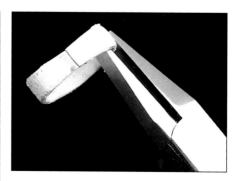

A ring ready for soldering, with a coating of "Argotec" to prevent fire staining.

Using Wire

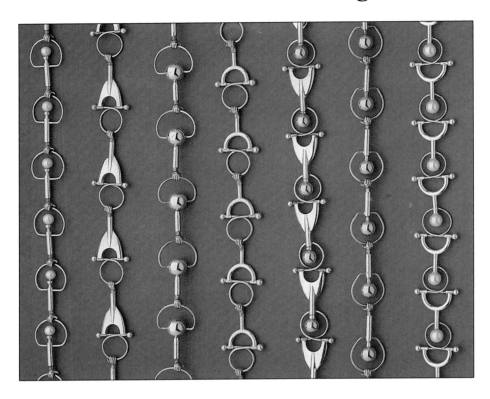

There are numerous uses for wire in jewellery making. It is supplied in a variety of sections:

◯ Round

△ Triangular

◠ Semicircular or D section

▢ Square

▭ Rectangular

⌐ Bearer

Wire with a hole through the centre is known as chenier. It is available in round and square sections with walls of different thicknesses. Wire is supplied in coils by weight and chenier comes in lengths. Wire and chenier can be drawn down to a smaller width by means of a suitable drawplate.

YOU WILL NEED

Copper and silver wire, 0.5–2mm
Round drawplate or other
   sectioned drawplates
Round-nose pliers
Half-round pliers
Flat-nose pliers
Hand drill and hook
Large serrated pliers
Vice

DRAWING DOWN WIRE

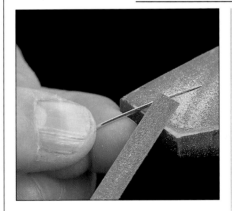

Drawing down D. Section wire.

1 File one end of a length of wire to a longish taper and then anneal it.

2 Find the size of hole in the drawplate that will take the taper, but not the full width of the wire, and push the taper through, gripping the end with the serrated pliers.

3 Pull the wire through the hole keeping it straight. Continue working down through the holes annealing

the wire as it becomes hard and difficult to work. Wire can be helped through the holes by rubbing a little beeswax along its length.

Hold the drawplate in the vice but take care not to close the jaws of the vice over any of the holes in the plate, which could burr or damage the fine edges.

DRAWING DOWN CHENIER

1 Take a length of wire that is longer than the chenier and that has a diameter the same as the inside diameter of the chenier.

2 Coat the wire with beeswax and pull it through the chenier to coat the inside walls with beeswax.

3 Replace the wire in the chenier and file one end to a taper.

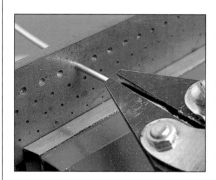

4 Pull the chenier through the drawplate as for wire, then remove the wire by pulling the protruding end of the wire through a hole in the drawplate that is too small for the chenier.

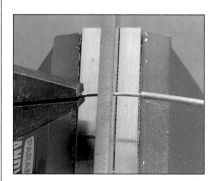

MAKING A JUMP RING

Jump rings are used for joining chains, loops and catches. They are supplied in most sizes, or you could order a selection of sizes. They are also very easy to make yourself.

1 Take a former of the appropriate size – the wrong end of a drill bit will do – and anneal the wire.

2 Put the former in the vice so that it is horizontal, protecting the cutting edge if you are using a drill bit.

3 Close the vice and grip the end of the wire with serrated pliers.

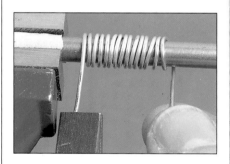

4 Wrap the other end of the wire around the former so that each coil fits snugly against the previous one, until the wire is finished. Take the former out of the vice.

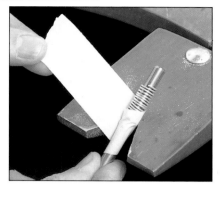

5 Snip off any protruding ends of wire and wrap masking tape round the wire while it is still on the former.

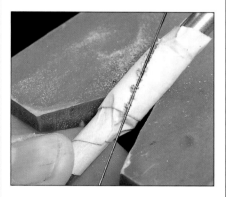

6 Pierce through the tape and wire, making a slightly diagonal line and taking care not to mark the former. Remove the tape.

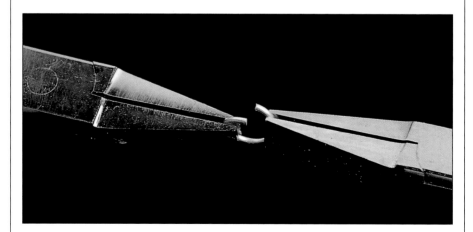

7 You can close the ends of a jump ring by taking a pair of flat-nose pliers in each hand. Hold the jump ring in one pair of pliers and use the other pair to adjust the other side of the jump ring with a twisting movement to close the ends together.

MAKING A BROOCH PIN

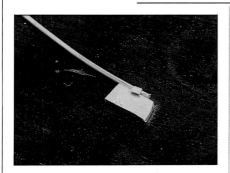

1 Make a silver tag from sheet silver; it should be slightly less thick than the inside of the fichu joint. Solder it to a length of 1mm round wire. File a groove along the top of the tag to make a good join.

2 Use a piercing saw to cut the wire to length and file the end into a good point. Gently tap the wire with your jeweller's hammer while you roll it (as far as the tag) on a smooth metal surface. This hardens the pin after soldering.

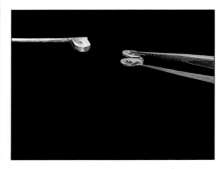

3 Drill a hole through the tag to align with the holes of the fichu joint.

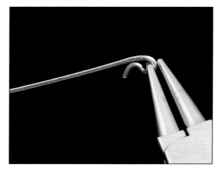

4 A pin can also be made by simply bending the wire. Do not anneal the wire – it will stay springy if it has not been heated.

TWISTING SILVER WIRE TOGETHER

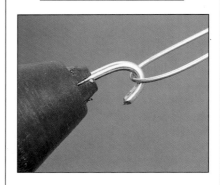

1 Take a piece of silver wire about 50cm long and fold it in half.

2 Fix the two ends into the vice and tighten it.

3 Take a hand drill and fix a hook in the chuck. Put the loop of silver wire over the hook and, keeping the wire taut, wind up the drill until the wire is twisted as far as you want. Remove the wire from the hook and the vice.

4 Put flux along the length of twisted wire, place paillons along its length or use a solder stick and solder it.

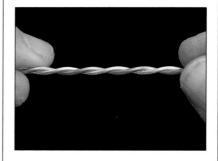

5 Try different combinations of wire. Use one length of copper and one of silver, or twist two smaller wires and then twist those with larger wires. Twist round wire with square wire. Try flattening the twisted wire, either with a hammer or through a rolling mill.

TWISTING WIRE

You can make fascinating combinations by twisting wires together. Wire will twist more evenly if it has been evenly annealed. You can either anneal the wire carefully with your torch or in a kiln at a temperature around 600–650°C for a minute or two. Alternatively, you can purchase soft annealed coils.

Twisted wire can be made into rings, loops for chains or earrings, used around the edge of a stone setting or as general decoration. Experiment!

There are many different chains you can buy from your supplier. These are usually quite fine and, for general purposes, they are difficult to improve upon. However, if you want a chain with larger links or one that is more interesting, try making one yourself. It is important that chain should move freely, so try to make sure that the links are free to move in all directions.

CHAINS

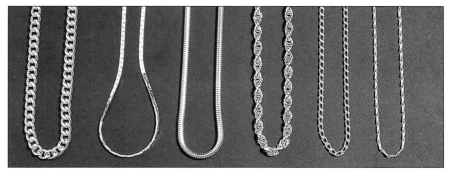

A selection of ready-made chains.

MAKING OVAL LINKS

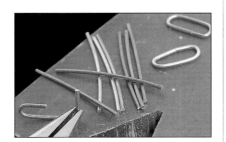

1 Cut several lengths of wire to the same length – 40mm, for example – bend up the ends and solder them together. Make them round by sliding them over a triblet or former and tapping them with a mallet.

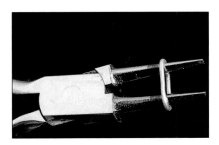

2 Take a pair of round-nose or flat-nose pliers. Place the loop over the plier ends, with the solder join at one end, and pull the pliers apart just enough to stretch the wire.

If you are making several links, mark the position on the pliers with tape or a red line so they are the same size.

MAKING RECTANGULAR LINKS

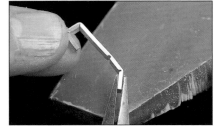

1 Cut several pieces of wire to length, allowing for the joins to be in the middle of the long sides. Use your dividers to mark each piece where the bends will be, then, with a triangular file, make a groove along the marked lines to slightly more than half the depth of the silver.

2 Carefully bend the wire with flat-nose pliers, apply flux and hard solder up all the corners.

MAKING LITTLE BALLS

Silver bracelet. Rebecca Smith.

1 Cut equal lengths of silver wire, approximately 3mm long, place them one at a time on your charcoal block and heat them until they run up into a ball.

MAKING UP A CHAIN

To make a chain pierce through the solder join of the links, open up the join enough to link into the next link. Close the link using flat nose pliers. Isolate each link to resolder the joint.

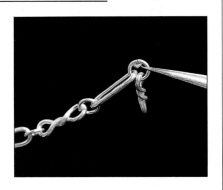

Filing

To achieve a good finish on silver, every scratch that is made has to be removed and replaced by a finer one. Do this by working systematically from coarse files, to needle files, to wet and dry papers, to the different grades of polish. At each stage you should check that you have erased the scratches from the previous tool.

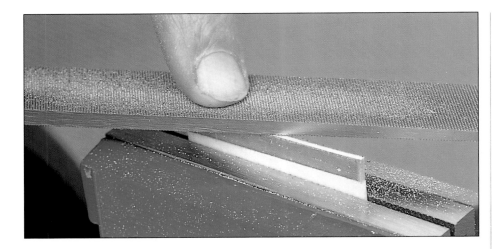

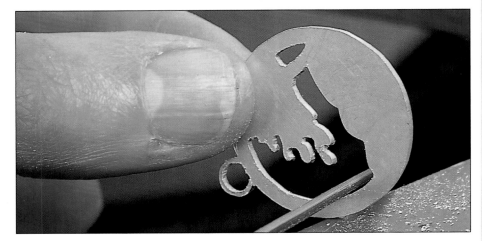

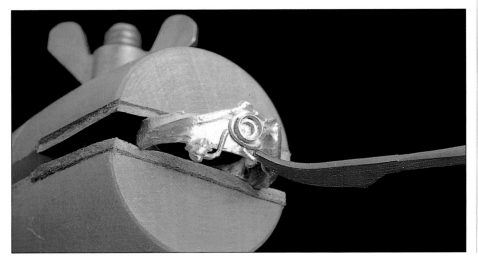

A file cuts in only one direction, and there are many different shaped files that will follow the line of your work. In general, use a flat file on a flat surface; an oval or half-round file on inside curves; a triangular file for grooves and small corners; a rectangular or square file for right angles; and a round file to cut U grooves and open out holes.

Some rectangular or flat files have a cutting edge, which is useful for making grooves, and some files have a safe edge, which allows you to file one surface without damaging another that is close to it.

FLAT FILING
When you are filing a long edge flat, hold the silver parallel in the safe jaws of the vice. Hold the flat file in one hand and move it diagonally in long smooth strokes along the silver, keeping it flat and straight with your index finger.

CURVES
On inside curves use an oval or half-round file, keeping it straight. Work on alternate sides of the work to keep the filing even.

RIFFLER FILES
These files have curved tips and a smooth centre that is used as the handle. They allow filing in difficult corners and on convex and concave surfaces.

From top: flat filing; filing an inside curve; and using a riffler file.

Texturing

You can add an interesting further dimension to your work by texturing all or some of the surfaces. Before you start to texture make sure that the surface is clean and free of grease. Some surfaces can be textured before piercing, but a simple matt or frosted finish is added after polishing.

YOU WILL NEED

Some or any of the following:
Planishing or flat-faced hammer
Selection of punches
Wet and dry papers, 240–600
Steel wool
Pendant motor with a selection of burr ends
Steel mop for polishing motor
Pitch

PLANISHING

Support your work on a polished stake or wooden former, and work around the piece with a smooth rhythmic action with your planishing hammer. This should be done on your finished piece, because the gentle tapping will slightly mark the surface. Do not hit too hard or you could alter the shape of your work.

USING A PUNCH

You can make your own patterns to achieve an interesting effect on your work by filing grooves into the end of a punch. The reverse pattern will appear on your work.

To do this take some tool steel stock, about 10cm long and 5–6mm square, and slightly taper both ends with your file. File your pattern into one end. Finish the ends by bevelling the corners so that the edges do not drag on your work. Harden the end by heating the punch up to cherry red and quickly quenching in cold water. Reheat the working end only with a soft flame until it becomes yellow. Quench again. This method will allow you to produce a whole range of different patterns yourself, although it is possible to buy different patterned punches.

To add texture with a punch: set your work by gently heating the pitch, dropping the work in it and, when it is slightly cooler, pushing the pitch with your fingers up round the edge of the work. First, dampen the ends of your fingers.

With your punch at an angle of 90° to your work, hit the top with a hammer and work it steadily around the area you want to mark. If the work starts to curl up out of the pitch, remove it, anneal and straighten it before replacing it in the pitch. When you have finished, gently heat the pitch around the work and use an old pair of pliers to prise up the edge of the work and lift it out. Pitch can be burnt off or dissolved in turpentine.

PENDANT MOTOR

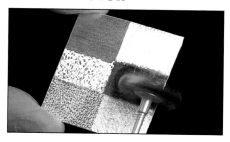

If you possess, or have access to, a pendant motor, there are all sorts of little burrs and cutters that can be used to produce different surfaces on silver. Try them out on a piece of scrap metal first to see what effect you prefer. It is also useful to get some practice with the tool before you start to texture a beautifully finished piece of work.

OTHER ABRADERS

Steel wool and wet and dry papers will give a good matt finish if they are rubbed over your finished work. Try them on scrap metal first to be sure of the effect. Use a circular motion or a forwards and backwards movement. If you have a polishing motor, you can fit a stainless steel mop, which also gives a matt finish.

Finishing and Polishing

Finishing work well will transform a rather dull-looking piece into something you will be proud of. The processes of polishing and finishing may take longer than you imagine, but if you complete each stage thoroughly, you will be well rewarded with the end result.

YOU WILL NEED

Some or all of the following:
Wet and dry papers
Polishing sticks
Chamois leather, dusters
Proprietary silver polish
Polishing strings
Lighter fuel
Pendant motor with mops and
    brushes
Polishing motor with hard,
    medium and soft mops
Cone for inside ring polishing

POLISHING BY HAND

An emery stick is used to give a sanded finish.

After completing the fine filing on your work, remove the filing marks by rubbing wet and dry papers over the surface. Begin with a fairly coarse paper – 240 or 400 – and work down to 600 and 1200, if necessary. As their name suggests, these papers can be used with or without water.

Make a polishing stick by gluing pieces of suede onto wooden sticks measuring approximately 300 × 20 × 10mm.

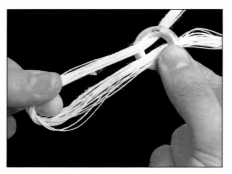

Polishing strings – use as many or as few as you need to reach difficult areas.

To polish inside difficult areas, keep some polishing strings hooked up in your workshop. Thread as many as necessary through the work and moisten them with lighter fuel, rub on the polish and rub the work along the string. The polishes required for both the sticks and the strings are:
▌ **Coarse** – Tripoli, which is a sticky brown block
▌ **Medium** – Hyfin, which is a finer white block
▌ **Fine** – rouge, which is a fine red round block.

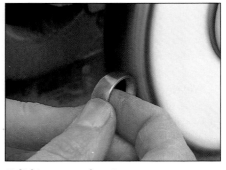

Polishing on an electric motor.

Remove any thick polish left on the surface with detergent and warm water before moving on to the next grade of polish. You will find it useful to have a chamois leather, spread out on a large, flat surface. You can rub the polishes on to it with lighter fuel.

POLISHING BY MACHINE
You will need separate mops for each polish – use a stiff mop for Tripoli, a softer brush or calico mop for Hyfin, and a soft sheepskin mop for rouge. Hard felt cones are used for the inside of rings.

CAUTION
Before you use a polishing motor, make sure that you have tied long hair back and that you have no loose clothing that could get caught in the revolving wheel.

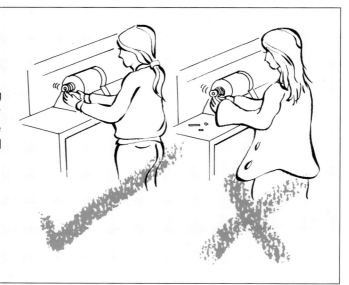

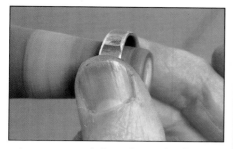

When you are polishing the inside of a ring on a felt cone, hold the ring firmly and rotate the ring so that all the inside edges come into contact with the cone.

With the motor running, press some polish onto the mop. Then hold the work to be polished between 4 and 5 o'clock on the mop. Do not place it above the centre line of the mop or the speed will whip your work out of your hands, with possible disastrous consequences. Use both hands to hold the work and push it towards the mop. Take care not to push the edges too hard because they can very quickly lose their crispness.

After each application of polish, clean your work with a detergent or in an ultrasonic cleaner.

To highlight edges or raised surfaces on a matt piece, rub them with a burnisher, using a little pressure. Remember to keep the burnisher polished to prevent it scratching your work.

OXIDIZING

After you have polished your work, you may feel that an area would look good with a black background. This can be oxidized, using a small piece of potassium sulphide – a cube about $10 \times 10 \times 10$mm dissolved in about 0.5l of boiling water. Immerse the piece in the liquid by hanging it from a piece of silver wire. Remove it after about a minute when it is a good black colour. The colour varies according to the time the item is immersed, and if the solution is too hot, flaking may result. You can now polish away any surface you have designed for highlights, but be careful if you are using a polishing mop not to remove the oxidized background. A burnisher can be used more selectively.

Oxidized silver earrings with gold decoration. Daphne Krinos.

Findings

Findings is the word used to describe the mechanical fittings that are attached to jewellery and that hold the piece to the body or to your clothing. Standard silver findings should always be used when you work with silver. Silver plate on base metals can soon wear away and may cause allergy problems. Manufacturer's catalogues include a good range of findings, but you will sometimes find it more appropriate to make your own. Always take care to position your findings so that your work is balanced correctly.

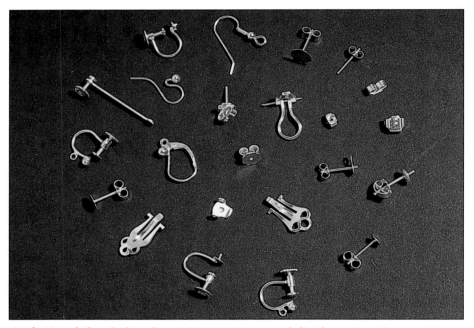

A selection of silver findings for earrings – ear screws and clips for unpierced ears, and ear hooks and wires with butterfly fittings for pierced ears.

A manufactured clip fitting.

NON-PIERCED EARS

If you are making earrings for non-pierced ears it is probably easier to buy fittings for clips or screw-type fittings. It is possible to pierce out the shape from sheet silver if you need a heavier gauge and then wire can be bent to fit.

EARRINGS

You can make earrings in several styles:

▌ Wire with butterfly fitting
▌ Wire hooks
▌ Hoops
▌ Clips.

PIERCED EARS

Cut pieces of round wire approximately 12mm long, file one end straight across and use easy solder to solder them to the earring. Taper the other end and, about one-third of the way up the pin, file a tiny groove round the diameter. Burnish the pin after rolling it along a metal surface, gently hammering to harden the silver. Add butterfly fittings.

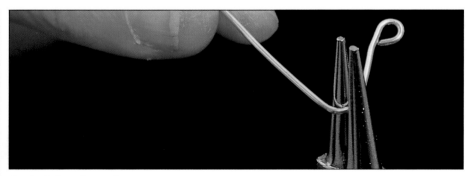

A wire is bent for ear loops.

To make loop earrings for pierced ears, bend up loops of wire using round or half-round pliers. Avoid soldering if possible, but if it is necessary, solder before bending and harden by tapping with the hammer as above.

To make hoops solder a 0.75mm wire to the end of thicker wire, and drill a hole the same size in the other end. Wrap the wire around the top of a mandrel and hit downwards until the hoop is springy and the correct size.

PINS AND BROOCHES

There is a large selection of brooch fittings you can buy. Some of these are very small, and it may be more appropriate to make your own. Making brooch pins is described in the section on wire. You can make your own catch by bending a piece of wire, of which you have tapered one end, and flattening the end that is to be soldered to the work. Make a fichu joint by cutting out a rectangle of silver approximately 15mm long by 5mm high, filing two grooves at 5 and 10mm and bending it up with flat-nose pliers. Run hard solder up the grooves, before soldering it to your work with easy solder.

CUFFLINKS

Attachment for chain to link onto a cufflink.

A "T" bar fitting – the V is soldered into position and the bar then riveted onto it.

To make a chain link fitting solder a half-round, using wire or piercing it out from a sheet, to the back of the cufflink and attach five links of chain that you have made or belcher chain. Then attach that to the opposite side of the link. You can combine a T-bar with a chain by attaching the chain to

a piece of thick round wire or chenier.

To fix a T-bar, solder the U or V shape at an angle to the link and attach the T-bar by means of a rivet after the soldering is completed.

NECKLACES, BRACELETS AND PENDANTS

Bolt ring.

The clasps you will use are:
▌ Bolt ring
▌ Box catch (see advanced techniques, page 92)
▌ Hook and eye
▌ Spring fitting (see advanced techniques, page 92)
▌ Riveted joint.

Bolt rings are the usual way of fastening manufactured chains. They come in different sizes and work well. After soldering leave to air cool, as the spring will become soft if it is quenched immediately.

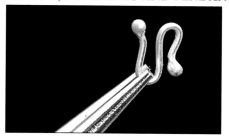

Wire for hook with both ends run up to make little balls.

A hook and eye fastening gives the greatest scope for your own creativity. A simple style can be made by heating both ends of a length of wire, approximately 40 × 1mm, so that the ends run up into balls. Hold the wire in your insulated tweezers, flux the ends and concentrate the flame on one end, with a charcoal block behind it. The end will run up into a ball as it begins to melt. Turn it over and repeat the process on the other end. Use round and half-round pliers to bend the wire into a long S shape. Solder up one end with easy solder, and curl the ball on the other end to turn up. Hammer the central area flatter on the anvil to harden it up and improve the appearance.

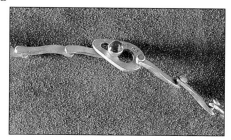

A sapphire was set into the end of this fastener to add interest to the back of the necklace.

Another way of achieving the same end is to pierce out an end tag, with a hole at the chain end going into a slit. Make the fastener by bending up a piece of wire the same diameter as the slit and soldering a silver ball to the top so that it will fit through the opposite hole.

Riveting

Silver can be joined together by means of a rivet. This is often useful if you are using other materials – wood, for example – which cannot be soldered.

Drill two holes of 1mm into silver 1.

Mark the position for holes on the wood 2 and silver 3, and drill.

Solder in two silver wires to fit the holes in silver 1.

Countersink the top of the holes in silver 3.

Place pieces 2 and 3 over the silver wires. Push down.

Cut wires to about 1.5mm above 3 and file flat.

Support the underside of 1 on the anvil.

Using a pointed punch, spread the tops of the wire pins by tapping gently a couple of times with a small hammer.

Take a flat-headed punch and continue to spread the top until it is firm. Neaten off with a file.

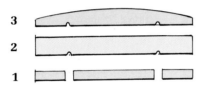

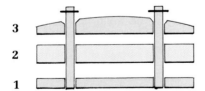

Drill through silver 4, wood 5 and silver 6 with a 1mm drill bit.

Take a length of annealed wire which fits snugly through the holes.

Cut each end of wire so that it protrudes approximately 1.5mm beyond silver pieces 4 and 6.

Countersink the holes at a and b.

Push both wires through the three thicknesses.

Support the end of the wire on the anvil.

Spread the head of the wire with a punch.

Turn it over and spread the other side.

File to neaten and clean with an emery cloth.

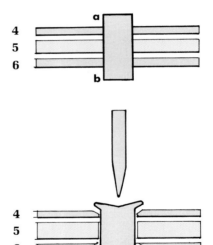

You should be able to file and polish the heads so that they disappear. If the head of the rivet is well spread it will sit into the countersink and be quite safe.

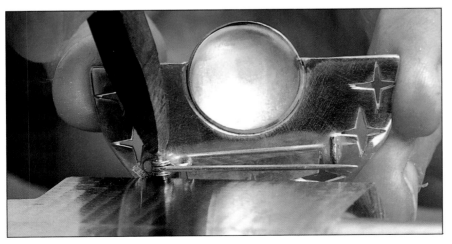

Doming and Shaping

Being able to shape your silver into round domes and U shapes gives an added depth to your work. A doming block is used for forming a disc of silver sheet into a dome or semisphere. A swage block is used for forming a strip of silver sheet into a U-shaped section. A sandbag is used to support the silver while it is being shaped with wooden or metal formers or punches. A lead block will give under the pressure of a punch but will retain the shape around it. Lead bits, if heated with silver, will result in disastrous holes, so always put paper or calico between silver and lead.

MAKING A DOME

YOU WILL NEED

Doming block
Wooden or steel punches
Sandbag
Swage block
Hammer

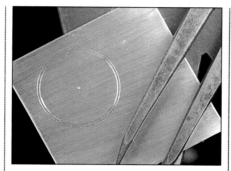

1 Cut a disc of silver. When you are piercing out a disc, mark the circle on the silver and then mark another circle about 1mm larger around it, pierce between the two lines and then file down to the first line.

2 Anneal the silver, then place it in the appropriate semisphere in the block. The disc should be slightly smaller than the diameter of the semisphere. With a punch to fit, hammer the silver into the semisphere. Make the dome as small as you need, annealing it when necessary.

MAKING A U SECTION

1 Lay a strip of silver down the largest groove of the swage block. Make sure that the silver is not wider than the groove.

2 Lay the side of an appropriate punch along the silver and hammer the punch with a wooden mallet to push the silver into the groove. Do not use a metal hammer, which will mark the punch.

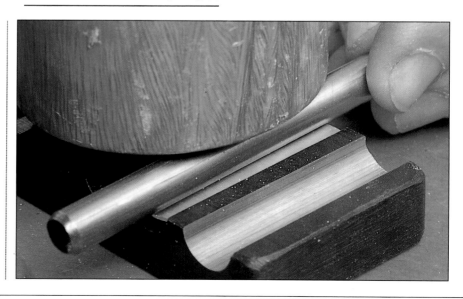

Other Materials

With a little inspiration, all sorts of interesting and inexpensive jewellery can be made by combining a variety of different materials with silver. Keep a collection of bits and pieces to experiment with in spare moments.

Turned walnut bowl with fine silver decoration. The silver is fixed to the wood with rivets. Jinks McGrath and Steve Turner.

Rosewood and silver bangle with matching ring. Jinks McGrath.

WOOD

Hardwoods are the most suitable to use with silver. There are, of course, sound environmental reasons for not using any hardwood in jewellery making, but it is possible to find wood such as ebony, which can be reclaimed from an old mirror or hairbrush. Boxwood, which grows readily, is an excellent light-coloured close-grained wood, as are lignum vitae (guaiacum), although it is rather oily, and rosewood. Wood can be attached with rivets, screws or a good glue. It can be pierced out using your piercing saw with one of the heavier blades, but you might find a coping saw easier on a large job. Edges can be filed and sanded, and rubbing beeswax or linseed oil over a finished piece will bring it to life.

Another way of using wood is to collect the dust produced by filing and sanding and mixing it into an epoxy resin. You can build up an image with different colours by filling the spaces between silver wires soldered to a framework with the wood and resin mixture. Leave it to dry, level off with a file and then sand until smooth. Any little holes can be filled with more resin mixture. Finally, oil the surface.

NATURAL STONE

A walk on the beach or in the country or a gentle stroll in a park can not only be a source of inspiration but is also an excellent source of natural stone. Some stones and pebbles will be harder and more durable than others, so try flaking and breaking them first to see whether they are worth using. Interesting pieces can be mounted in silver or wrapped in silver wire and then linked up to make an attractive pattern within the overall piece. Alternatively, you can buy wonderful ready-cut pieces of agate from good stone dealers, who often also offer other unusual shapes, which can be used to make intriguing jewellery.

PAPIER MÂCHÉ

Make little papier mâché balls or oblongs, paint them, give them a coat of varnish and drill through the middle so they can be hung on necklaces or earrings.

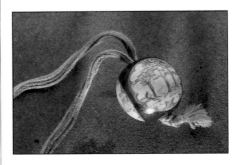

A finely-painted ball hung onto silk threads. Paul Vincent.

ACRYLICS

Perspex sheets can be bought in a variety of thicknesses and colours, and companies that make or use large quantities of plastic can be generous with their offcuts. Use a coping saw for most of the cutting out, as the heat that is generated will soon clog a small piercing saw blade. Perspex can be filed, sanded, polished and buffed up with metal polishes. It can be set into silver, riveted and screwed, but a special plastic adhesive should be used when gluing as most ordinary adhesives alter the surface of the acrylic. Perspex can be heated in a warm domestic oven (about 100°C/212°F) and bent to shape. Be careful not to overheat, which will cause air bubbles within the plastic. Resins are used for cold-cast enamelling. Colours are mixed with the resin and a catalyst, and the liquid is poured into depressions or cells in the silver. If you are casting resin into a framework that does not have a metal back, place the frame on an oiled sheet or mould.

GLASS

Clear glass or pebbles can be used as the basis for colourful painted designs. Use enamel paints and cover them with a coat of protective varnish. You can make a very original necklace by collecting interesting shapes and holding them in a silver framework. Small pieces of coloured glass can be inlaid and glued into silver cells to build up a mosaic, or use glass beads, mixed in with silver beads, to make attractive earrings and necklaces.

1 **Cast acrylic on top of a painted base makes these pieces very colourful. Rowena Park.**

2 **Little paintings on clear glass joined with silver wire and tiny beads. Nancy Church.**

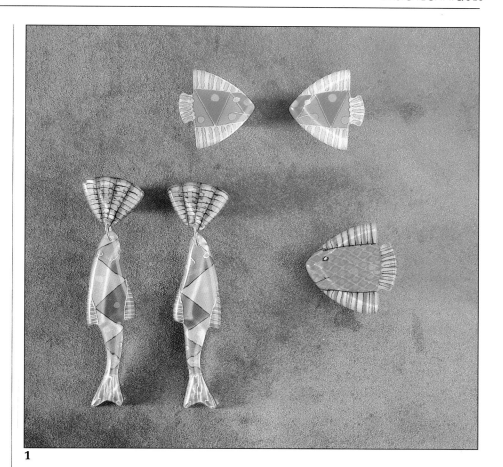

1

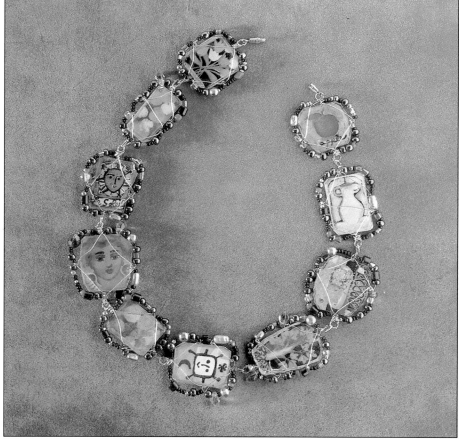

2

FINDINGS

Findings for use with other materials are much the same as those already described for use with silver. Most will have to be glued or riveted in position, but if possible design your piece so that the fitting can be soldered to the silver sheet first.

NECKLACE THREADS

For a flexible necklace made of different materials, threads are often used instead of wire or chain.

Silk threads are used for stringing pearls, freshwater pearls and semi-precious beads. The drilled pearls or beads are threaded onto the silk strands with a fine needle made from very fine brass wire, doubled and twisted together. After each pearl is added, make a knot in the silk to prevent them wearing each other away and from all falling off if the threads break. The silk is joined to the catch at the back by threading a fine spring gimp over the threads and through the jump ring on the catch; this prevents wear at the point of contact. The silk is then threaded back through the last three or four pearls and knotted again. The knot is coated with a transparent glue and made as small as possible so that it does not impede the flow of the pearls.

Nylon is used for threading other beads as long as they are not too heavy. The nylon is knotted at the ends only and held in little findings called calotte crimps, which close down over the glued and knotted end of the nylon. The calotte crimps are then linked to the fasteners. Alternatively, the nylon threads can be knotted directly onto the fastener.

Leather thread is used for very large beads. Tie the ends together with a bow or knot or fit a spring coil over the ends.

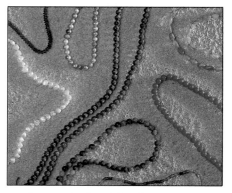

A selection of colourful and semi-precious beads. Marcia Lanyon.

Tiger tail (very strong thread) is a stronger but less flexible way of hanging beads. It has the advantage that it will not lose its shape. It cannot be knotted, so it is looped at both ends, and the loop is kept in place by means of a crimping bead. The loose ends of the thread are then tucked back through the beads. The fastener is attached to the tiger tail loop. If the beads are not heavy enough for tiger tail it may kink.

TITANIUM

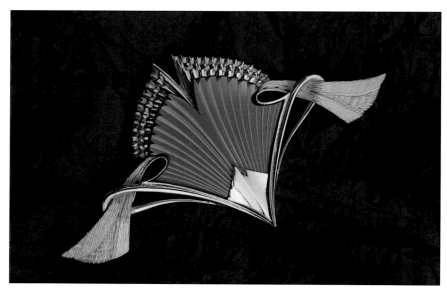

Coloured titanium set into a brooch. Brian Eburah.

This light, grey metal, which is extremely strong, is used in jewellery mainly because of the attractive range of colours that appear after heat treatment. Because it is so hard, piercing should be done with a strong blade, and it takes longer than piercing silver. Titanium should not be rolled down in your rolling mill, and it cannot be soldered, shaped or forged. It is, therefore, either set like a stone into, or riveted onto, a piece of work. Before heating titanium, clean the surface by rubbing it with wet and wet dry papers and de-greasing it with an ammonia-based detergent. Small particles of titanium are combustible, so do not file, saw or clean it near a naked flame.

Heat can be applied with a torch all over a piece or concentrated locally to produce a spectacular range of colours. After heating, titanium should be left in the air to cool. The colours will remain: they appear as a result of the film of oxides, produced by the heat, on the surface. Light passes through the film and is then refracted from the surface of the metal to produce all colours of the spectrum. After colouring, designs or lines can be scribed with a diamond-mounted scriber.

Simple Rub-over Stone Settings

A piece of jewellery can be greatly enhanced by the addition of a well-chosen stone. There are many ways of setting stones to show them off to their best advantage – large, opaque stones look best with a simple rub-over setting, for example, and most faceted stones (those with flat-polished faces) are enhanced by an open-back setting which allows the light to reflect around the stone. When you use a stone or stones, try to design a piece around them. Carefully consider the sort of setting you need and work with that in mind. Some stones are softer than others and are best set so that they are not constantly vulnerable. Stone dealers have a host of stones to choose from, so have a good look before you make your selection. In this section we deal with a basic setting; other setting techniques are explained from page 82 to 87.

YOU WILL NEED

Some or all of the following:
Silver sheet
Bearer wire
Small flat punch
Hammer
Setter's wax
Ring vice
Burnisher
Suede stick
Round and half-round pliers
Triblet
Graver

RUB-OVER SETTING FOR ROUND STONES

Measure the diameter of your stone – 8mm, for example – and use the calculation $2\pi r$ to find the circumference of the stone

$(\pi = \frac{22}{7}$ or 3.141): $2 \times \frac{22}{7} \times 4 = 25.14$

The silver surrounding the stone is known as the bezel. Choose a thickness of silver that is appropriate to the size of the stone to make the bezel. Generally, use the thinnest silver that is practicable. Silver that is too thick can detract from the stone and can be hard to push over. In this case, if the stone has a diameter of 8mm, a thickness of about 0.6mm is right. To find the length of the bezel add together the circumference of the stone and 1½ times the thickness of the silver:

$$25.14 + (0.6 \times 1.5) =$$
$$25.14 + 0.9mm = 26.04$$

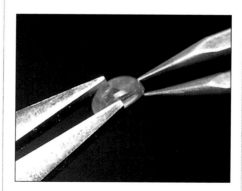

1 Measure the height with a pair of dividers. Mark this height on your silver by laying the dividers on a straight edge of the silver and running them along the surface.

2 Mark out the length you need, making sure that both ends are square. Pierce out the silver and anneal it. With your half-round pliers, bend the two ends up so that they meet exactly. At this stage there is no need to make the shape round. To keep the shape tight for soldering, push the two ends past each other and then spring them back into position. Solder the ends together using hard solder.

3 Make the bezel round by tapping it on your triblet or in your pliers. File off any excess solder from the inside.

4 Check that the stone fits. It should not be necessary to force the stone to fit; it should just slip in. A small gap all round is acceptable. If the bezel is too

---

STONE SETTING
The height of the bezel should be about one-third the height of the stone. However, look at the stone and note where the curve actually starts, for this is where your bezel should rest to hold the stone down.

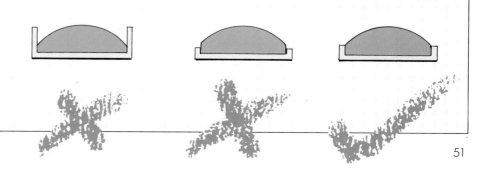

small pierce it open at the solder seam and add in a piece of the same silver used for the bezel. Solder it up again. If the bezel is too big pierce it open at the solder seam, cut out a piece and try the stone. Resolder the join.

5 Rub the bottom of the bezel on a flat file to make sure it sits perfectly straight, then place the bezel on a piece of silver between 1 and 1.5mm thick. Flux the silver and solder it. You can use medium solder, but if you have much more soldering to do on your piece it may be better to use hard solder. Place the paillons round the outside edge of the bezel and heat the surrounding silver before bringing the heat onto the bezel.

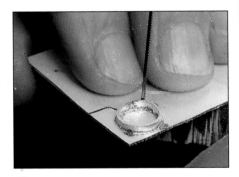

6 After pickling and rinsing, cut away the excess silver from the outside of the bezel. File the outside edge and clean it with wet and dry papers. The bezel is now ready to add to your piece.

7 If you need an open setting so that the light brings out the best qualities in your stone, cut away most of the back. Place one side of the dividers on the outside of your setting and the other side inside the bezel. Scribe a line round the circumference,

leaving a margin of about 2mm of silver on the inside. Drill a hole in the centre of the setting and pierce up to the line to cut away the inside. Neaten the edge with a needle file.

RUB-OVER SETTING FOR OVAL STONES

To find the length of the bezel add together the length and width of the stone, divide by 2 and multiply by π

$$\left(\pi = \frac{22}{7} \text{ or } 3.141\right).$$

For example:

$(8mm + 6mm) \div 2 \times 3.141 = 21.98$ or $= 22mm$

Add the length of the bezel to $1\frac{1}{2}$ times the thickness of the silver. If you are using 0.6mm silver, the calculation will be: $22 + 0.9mm = 22.9$ or $= 23mm$.

1 Cut out a strip of silver 23mm long; and the width necessary for your stone. Anneal the metal, bring the two ends together and solder. File off any excess solder from inside the bezel and tap it into shape on a triblet.

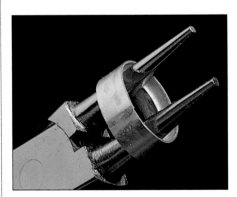

2 Using your round-nose pliers and with the join of the bezel at the side, slip the bezel over the pliers and pull it to form an oval. If you have an oval triblet, put the bezel onto the triblet and tap it into shape with a wooden mallet.

3 Check that the bezel fits the stone and adjust it as for the round bezel. Proceed as for the round bezel.

SETTING THE STONE

After all the work is completed on the piece and it has been polished up to the "Hyfin" stage, you are ready to set the stone.

1 Hold a ring in a ring vice and set a brooch or neckpiece into setter's wax or pitch. Leave the wax or pitch to harden, because the work must be really steady.

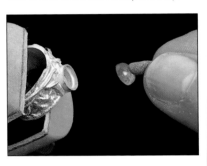

2 File the top edge of the bezel so that it is smooth and flat and clean off any file marks with wet and dry paper. Use either a stone holder or a piece of plasticine to hold the stone and place it in the setting.

3 Using a straight or curved highly polished burnisher, press over the edge of the setting at 12 o'clock, move down to 6 o'clock, then across to 9 o'clock followed by 3 o'clock. Continue pressing with a smooth motion all the way round until the whole circumference is pressed down onto the stone. The bezel rocker is used in a similar way except that a rocking motion is used to push against the bezel.

Simple rub-over settings. Daphne Krinos.

4 On heavier settings it is necessary to use a small punch with a hammer. Work in the same order as with a burnisher, gently tapping the punch at an angle of about 45° until all the bezel is resting on the stone. Take care not to mark the silver outside the bezel with the corner of the punch because deep marks are difficult to remove.

If the top surface of the setting has become uneven, either work gently round with the engraver to flatten it, and leave a shiny surface, or file it round, taking care not to mark the stone. After setting with a punch, a fine needle file will remove the marks of the punch, and the setting can then be polished with a suede stick.

SETTING UNCUT AND IRREGULARLY SHAPED STONES

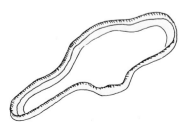

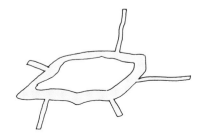

A simple rub-over setting can be made for a smooth stone by making a bezel to fit the shape of the stone, soldering the bezel to a base, and cutting away as much of the base as possible, leaving just enough for the stone to be supported.

A setting for a stone with an irregular surface can be made by cutting out a shape in which the bottom of the stone can sit from fairly thin silver and including different length prongs to hold the stone in place.

A conical stone can be set by wrapping wires either snugly or loosely round the stone. Start at the top and leave an end length turned into a loop. Wrap the other end around the stone as you want, and bring it back up to the top where it can be wrapped round the loop to tighten it. Cut off the wire and file the ends smooth.

Uncut stones

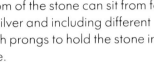

pink tourmaline crystal   **ruby crystal**   **blue topaz crystal**   **fluorspar crystal**   **tanzanite crystal**   **amber rough**

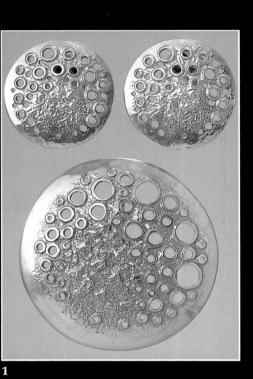

1

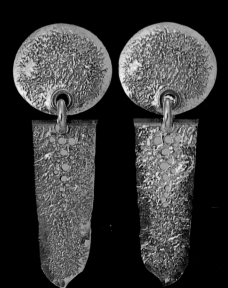

3

1 Reticulated earrings
and brooch with
pierced holes. Alan
Vallis.

2 Reticulated earrings.
Alan Vallis.

1

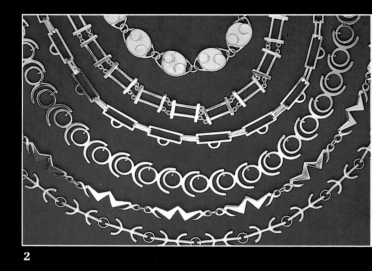

2

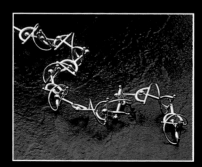

3

4

1 Textured necklace with
   carnelian. Alan Vallis.

2 Silver chains. Jinks
   McGrath.

3 Textured silver earrings
   with gold tips set with
   enamelled domes and
   moonstones. Jinks
   McGrath.

PROJECT Silver Ring Set with Oval Lapis Lazuli

TO MAKE THE RING

YOU WILL NEED

Ring sizer
Triblet
Binding wire
Wire cutters
Ruler
Silver sheet (80 × 20 × 1.2mm)
Ring template
Files
Flux and solder
Bearer wire (40 × 5mm)
Lapis lazuli (14 × 10mm)
Polish
Ring clamp or vice
Burnisher or punch and hammer
Wet and dry papers

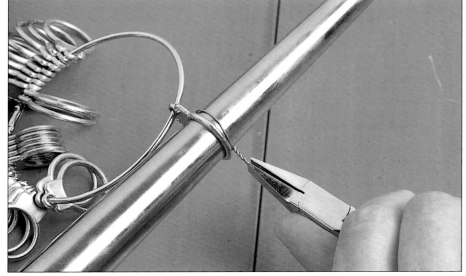

2

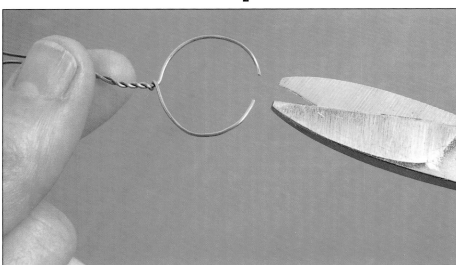

3

1 Measure the finger with ring sizers; I have made size 0.

2 Slide your ring sizer over the triblet. Cut a length of binding wire, wrap it around the triblet next to the ring sizer and twist it firmly.

3 Take the wire off the triblet, make a cut in it and straighten it out.

4 Measure the length of the wire against your ruler.

5 Add to the length of the wire 1½ times the thickness of the silver you are going to use for the ring.

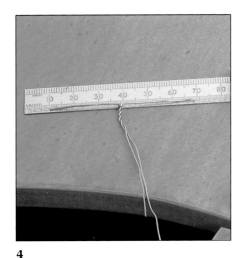

4

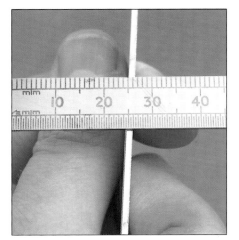

5

6

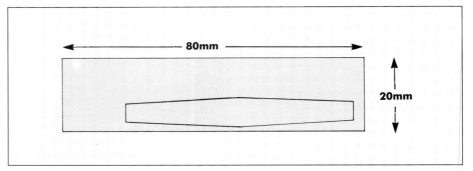

6 Trace the pattern for the ring shank using the template, adjust the length to fit, and transfer the design to the silver. Pierce it out.

7 File off the square edges on both the inside and outside with a flat and oval file and leave the ends flat.

8 Anneal, quench, rinse and dry the silver.

9 Bend up the ends of the silver and fit them closely together, although it is not necessary for the ring to be round at this stage.

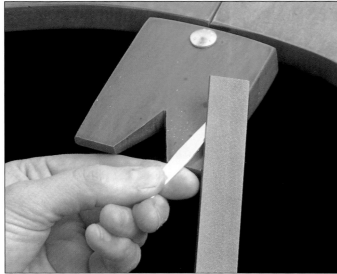

7

10

10 Flux the join and solder with hard solder. Quench, rinse and dry.

11 File off any excess solder from the inside of the ring. Make the ring round on the triblet and file off excess solder from the outside.

9

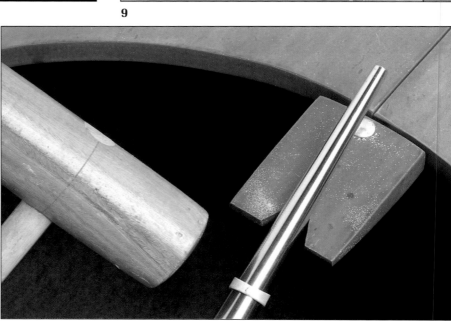

11

TO MAKE THE SETTING

Because the setting is being soldered to a curved surface, the bezel must be made to fit both the stone and the curve of the ring. I therefore used bearer wire for the setting.

1 Calculate the length of the bezel.

$$(14 + 10) \div 2 \times \pi = 37.7mm$$

Add 1½ times the thickness of the base edge of the bearer wire

$$1.5 + 37.7 = approx. 39.5mm$$

2 Cut off the required length of wire. Anneal, quench, rinse and dry.

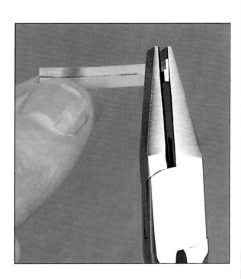

3 Bend up the ends to fit, flux the join and solder using hard solder. Quench, rinse and dry.

4 Make the setting oval. Check that the stone fits and make any necessary adjustments.

TO MAKE THE SETTING FIT THE RING

1 Use an oval file to file the base of the setting to fit the curve of the ring until it sits snugly on top.

2 Make sure the ring and setting are clean, flux the bottom of the setting and secure it to the ring with binding wire.

3 Solder the two together with easy solder. Pickle and rinse. Clean the ring with pumice paste.

4 File away any excess solder with a needle file, then work down through grades of wet and dry (used dry) papers.

5 Polish the ring, first with Tripoli, then with Hyfin. Polish the inside of the ring by hand or on a ring cone. Hold the ring in both hands while you polish it.

TO SET THE STONE

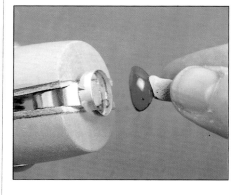

1 Hold the shank of the ring in a ring clamp or in the safe jaws of your vice. Place the stone in the setting.

2 Use your burnisher to push down on the two longer ends and then at the two sides. Continue rubbing all round the setting until it rests snugly over the stone. If you find that the silver is too hard to push over with a burnisher, use a punch and hammer in the same sequence.

3 Clean the setting and then polish the whole ring with jeweller's rouge, taking care not to get polish on the stone.

PROJECT Set of Earrings and Brooch

YOU WILL NEED

Silver sheet (0.5 × 30 × 35mm for domes; 1 × 50 × 65mm and 80 × 10 × 0.5mm for settings)
Texturing equipment
Scriber
Files
Moonstones (one 18mm across and two 12mm across)
Templates
Drill
Triblet
Flux and solder
Charcoal block
Polish
Fichu joint or silver fitting 1 × 10 × 3mm (for brooch)
Pliers
Safety catch or 1mm round silver wire (for brooch)
0.75–0.8mm silver wire (for ear stud and for ear loop)
Burnisher
Vice
Insulated tweezers
Jeweller's wax or pitch
Punches and hammer
Doming block

TO MAKE TEXTURED DOMES

1 Take a piece of silver sheet 0.5 × 30 × 35mm and texture the surface. The silver used here was planished over a doming block. On the reverse side of the silver mark three circles, one with a diameter of 20mm and two with diameters of 12mm. To make the piercing easier, scribe a slightly larger circle around the outside of each one and pierce between the lines. File to the inner line. Anneal, quench, rinse and dry.

2 Place the 20mm diameter circle, textured side down, on your doming block. The dome should be slightly larger than the circle. Use a wooden or metal punch, the same size as the dome, to punch the metal down. Repeat the process with smaller domes until the circle measures approximately 18mm across. Do the same with the two 12mm diameter circles until they measure approximately 10mm across.

30mm **35mm**

TO MAKE SETTINGS FOR STONES

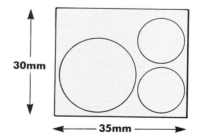

The bezel lengths are cut for the settings.

1 Use the silver sheet measuring 80 × 10 × 0.5mm to cut out three strips for the settings. These should be approximately 38.5mm long for the 12mm stones and 57.5mm long for the 18mm stones.

2 To determine the width of the settings, measure one-third of the height of the stones. These will make open settings when soldered to the surrounds.

TO MAKE
THE SURROUNDS

1 Take the silver sheet measuring 1 × 50 × 65mm and transfer the pattern of the earrings and brooch to it. Drill small holes in the centre of each star and pierce out.

2 Pierce out the shape of the surrounds, leaving the bottom edges straight for the time being.

3 If you are using textured domes, place these on the pierced out pattern, scribe closely around the outside of the dome, then scribe another line approximately 2mm inside the first line. Pierce out that circle, file and clean the edges.

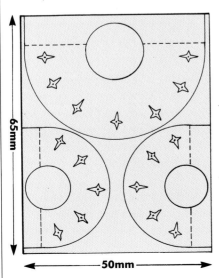

SOLDERING

1 Use hard solder to solder the bezels for the stones and make them round on your triblet.

2 Place the bezels in the correct position on the surrounds, add flux and place paillons of hard solder around the outside of the joins. Solder, quench, rinse and dry.

3 Make open settings for the stones by piercing away the backs of the settings. Remember to leave enough silver for the stones to sit on.

4 Place the textured domes in position, flux, place small paillons of hard solder around the joins and solder.

5 Working on the larger surround first, heat the surround, then bring the flame onto the setting or dome so that the solder runs. Repeat for the other two surrounds. Pickle, rinse and dry before cleaning with pumice powder. Now pierce along the bottom straight edge and close round the domes or bezels. File the edges neat.

MAKING THE
BROOCH FITTINGS

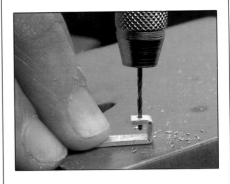

1 You can either buy a fichu joint or make one from silver 1 × 10 × 3mm. Use a triangular needle file to make two straight lines up the silver, 4mm from each end. Bend up the corners with flat-nose pliers and run hard solder into them. Drill a hole about 1mm wide in the centre of each side and file a small notch in the centre of the middle section.

2 Either buy a safety catch or make one from 1mm round wire, filed down at one end to a point. Use half-round or round-nose pliers to bend the wire into a loop. Bring the other end round to sit on the silver. File the bottom edge of the wire flat to ensure good contact.

FINDINGS FOR THE EARRINGS

1 Find the balancing point by placing the earring (and stone or textured dome) on the edge of a metal rule or file. Mark the position.

2 To make an ear stud cut a piece of 0.75–0.8mm silver wire and file straight across one end. Add flux and run a piece of easy solder on to it. Place some flux and a paillon of easy solder on the position you marked on the earring and position the earring on the soldering block, heating it through until the solder begins to run. Hold the wire pin in insulated tweezers and bring it down onto the work. Watch the solder flow while you hold it in position. Pickle, rinse and clean with pumice powder. File the wire to a point, clean with papers and burnish.

3 Make a loop using 0.75mm silver wire and form it into a jump ring with hard solder. Flatten the soldered side by holding about three-quarters of the ring in the safe jaws of a vice or in parallel pliers and tapping the protruding section with a hammer until it is flat. Put flux and a paillon of easy solder on the point you marked on the earring (place it above or below a star if necessary), place the earring on the soldering block and heat through until the easy solder starts to run. Hold the ring in the insulated tweezers, bring it down on the work and hold it in position while you watch the solder flow. Pickle, rinse and clean with pumice powder. Fix an ear wire to the loop after polishing and setting the stone.

CLEANING AND POLISHING

After pickling and rinsing the brooch and earrings, clean them carefully with pumice paste. File away all excess solder, covering any textured areas with masking tape if necessary. Work through the grades of wet and dry (used dry) papers to remove any scratches. Hold the pieces in both hands to polish them, first with Tripoli polish. Remove any traces of polish with detergent before using Hyfin. Set the stones and finally polish with jeweller's rouge.

SOLDERING THE BROOCH FITTINGS

1 Place the fichu joint in position on the silver, making sure that the brooch will sit correctly. Flux the join and place paillons of easy solder at each corner. Flux the underside of the safety catch – if you are using a bought catch, make sure that no flux runs up the inside – and run a paillon of easy solder onto it.

2 Place some flux and a paillon of easy solder where you want the safety catch to be. It should be at a slight angle to the fichu joint to give a firmer hold for the pin. Hold the safety catch in a pair of insulated tweezers and flux the bottom again.

3 Support the work in a charcoal block and heat it slowly, making sure that the large area of silver is heated before you bring the flame onto the fichu joint for the solder to run. As the solder runs for the safety catch, lower it onto the work and hold it steady. Remove the flame, still holding it steady, then pickle. Rinse, dry and clean with pumice powder.

SETTING THE STONES

1 Before you set the stones, make sure the work is held securely in pitch or in jeweller's wax. Gently heat the pitch or wax and place your work in it. Allow the pitch or wax to cool slightly, then gently work it up around the edges of the piece.

2 Set the stones using either a punch and hammer or a burnisher.

3 Play a gentle flame around the edge of your work to soften the pitch or wax, and carefully prise up the piece with tweezers. Avoid playing the flame directly onto the stone. Remove excess pitch with turpentine and excess wax with acetone.

2

ATTACHING THE BROOCH PIN

Make the tag of the pin (see page 38) to fit the inside of the fichu joint, and rivet the pin in place.

OXIDIZING THE TEXTURED DOME

If you want to oxidize the textured dome, protect all the other parts of the work with beeswax or stop-out varnish. Immerse all the pieces in a hot solution of potassium sulphide for about a minute, suspending them on fine silver wire attached to the fittings.

If oxidization occurs on areas that you had hoped to keep shiny, heat the whole piece up gently and quench in acid, which will eliminate the problem. However, you will have to start again with the potassium sulphide. Small areas of oxidization may be removed by careful polishing – preferably by hand – and you can bring highlights to the domes by gently rubbing them with the burnisher.

The finished pieces

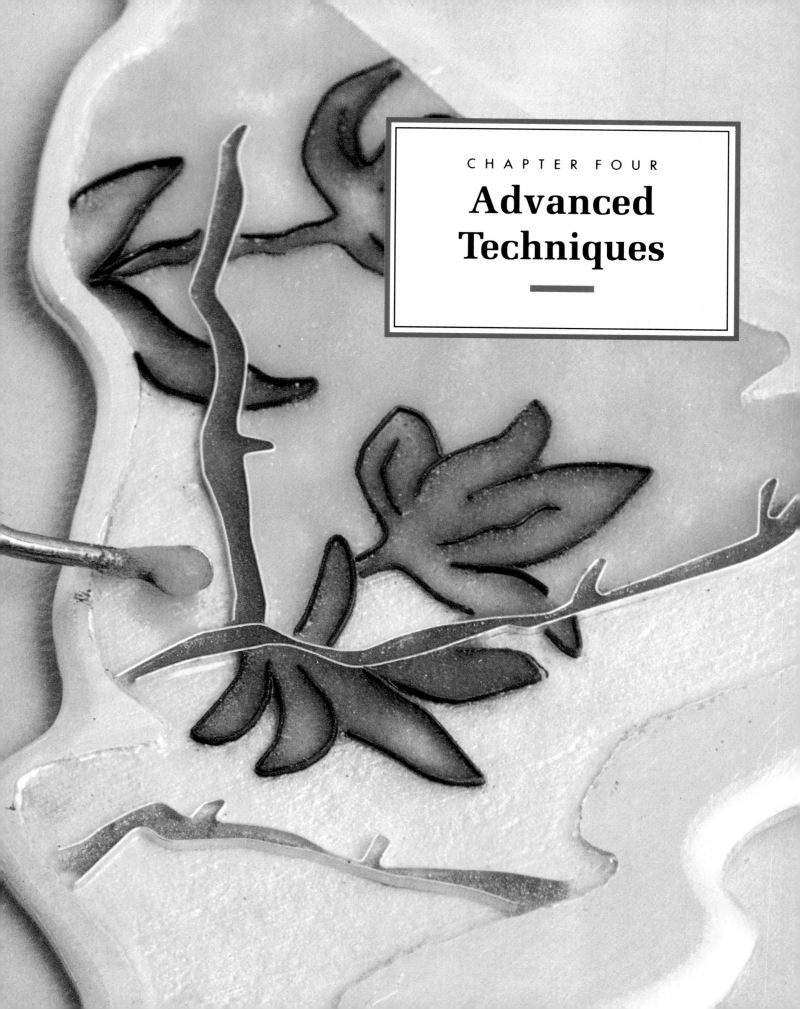

CHAPTER FOUR

Advanced Techniques

This section introduces some additional techniques of jewellery making. You may find all of them useful, or perhaps only one or two. Each of these techniques could be the subject of a book, and only if you decide to concentrate on one or two of them will you become fully familiar with all the intricacies of that particular technique. You can, of course, incorporate any of the techniques into a piece of work, and as you look through them you may be able to decide which suits your way of working. It would then be worth reading other, more detailed books on that subject. If you do not have access to all the equipment necessary for these techniques, join a jewellery class.

Forging

A piece of work that has been forged has a special quality that cannot be achieved in any other way than by the skilful use of hammers, heat and stakes. Forging gives a subtlety of shape and outline, and allows bends and twists to flow freely through the work. The silver is shaped by being pushed and compressed by hammers against the stakes, which widens and lengthens it.

1 Metal stakes which fit into an anvil.
2 Stake with different heads, held in the vice.
3 Metal heads held in a vice or anvil.
4 Lead block with depressions.

YOU WILL NEED
Good selection of stakes
Anvil
Steel block
Lead block
Raising hammer
Forming hammer
Chasing hammer
Planishing hammer
Half-round and round pliers
Flat-nose pliers

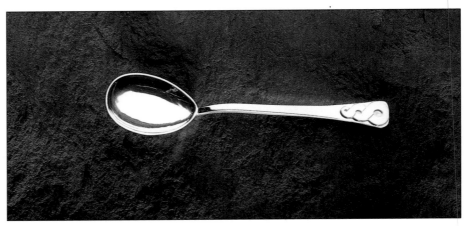

Forged spoon. Anton Pruden.

A silver disc is shaped on a wooden block.

Large, free-standing wooden blocks are used for blocking and working up a shallow dish. Dips or depressions are made in the wood, against which shape the edge of the piece is formed, gradually working the shape to the centre. All equipment used for forging should be kept clean, dry and lightly polished. Stakes can be ground to suit your particular needs, and while you are forging, wipe the hammer head and stakes to remove any particles that might otherwise become embedded in them and thereby mark the silver.

When you are shaping silver, keep the area being worked with the hammer or mallet in direct contact with the stake.

When silver is hit with hammers it must be supported at all times. Stakes are, therefore, chosen to produce the desired outline. The hammers move the silver in

different directions – some compress and others push – but all hammering is done rhythmically and precisely to maintain the same thickness of silver throughout.

To begin with make a simple chain from round wire of 1.5–2.5mm, forging each link. Anneal the wire and make sure that the

The ends of round wire are forged to make a chain.

hammer and steel block are clean and free from marks. Cut several pieces of wire 20–30cm long, hold one end flat on the block and begin hitting the wire from about one-third of the way up. Hit out towards the tip to spread the wire. Turn it around and hit the other end in the same way. Neaten the edges with a file and either solder a link on either end or drill a hole to take a jump ring.

You could try forging square wire into necklace links. Simply flatten the ends as for the round wire, hold one end in the safe jaws of the vice and the other end in your flat-nose pliers and twist through 180°.

Silver must be kept well annealed throughout the process. If it becomes hardened it will crack and split, which is difficult to correct. After the last solder, which will probably be a finding, leave the piece to cool in air instead of quenching to help to keep it hard. Any oxides and flux can be removed by placing the work in warm pickle.

A technique known as simulated forging enables you to forge the ends of your work so that they do not become thinner than the main area. This is achieved by soldering a double thickness of sheet silver to the end of the wire or sheet and then flattening and widening the end to shape. It is then filed and polished.

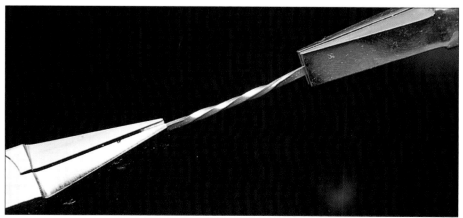

Square wire is twisted for chain links.

Engraving

Engraving is a method of cutting lines into silver to form patterns, pictures and initials. It requires many hours of practice to master the art of manoeuvring the engraving tool, and within the jewellery trade it is a highly specialized skill. However, it is possible to learn to engrave simple outlines and shapes, which will be useful to you alongside your other skills.

YOU WILL NEED

Arkansas stone and oil
Jeweller's wax and wood block
Pitch bowl
Basic cutters and handles

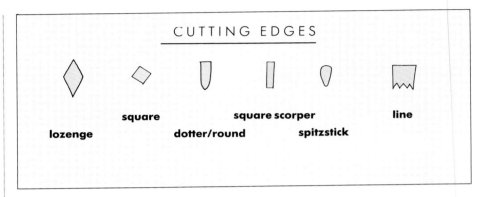

CUTTING EDGES

lozenge   square   dotter/round   square scorper   spitzstick   line

A professional engraver will have many different cutting edges to hand, but there are some basic shapes that will produce a good simple range of cuts. Practise on inexpensive metals such as copper, because it is difficult to control the tool at first.

An engraving tool (or graver) is a steel rod shaped into a specific shape at the tip and with the other end hammered into a wooden handle. Before it is used, the graver is ground and sharpened to the desired outline and when in use is kept sharpened on an oiled Arkansas stone. The point is angled away at 45°. Most engraving tools have a handle with one flat side so that it can be

Engraving the inside of a ring.

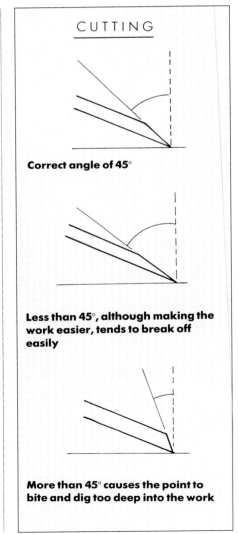

CUTTING

Correct angle of 45°

Less than 45°, although making the work easier, tends to break off easily

More than 45° causes the point to bite and dig too deep into the work

The large selection of graving tools used in the engraver's workshop.

held almost flat to the work without the handle getting in the way. The handle is tucked into the palm of the hand, with the tip of the graver protruding beyond the extended thumb and forefinger by about 2cm. The work should be held firmly either by melting jeweller's wax onto a wood block and dropping the heated work into it, or by holding it in the pitch bowl, which can be rotated on its wooden base. There are also special rotating hand-held blocks to hold work while it is being engraved.

To start the cut the graver is placed almost vertically to the work and then lowered and pushed along the line for 2–3cm before being lifted up slightly to flick away the silver. The thumb of the hand holding the tool acts as a sort of brake, and the other hand holds the work and pushes slightly in the opposite direction, turning it as necessary in the direction of the cuts. The engraving hand need hardly move at all. The thumb of the hand holding the work can rest against the other to help control, but keep it out of the line of the tool – a slip could cause a nasty cut. If the graver slips accidentally on the work, careful use of wet and dry papers or a curved burnisher and washing-up liquid rubbed around the scratch can rectify the error. If the cut is very deep, it may be easier to adapt your design to accommodate it.

Engraving tools can also be used to remove areas of silver before enamelling or before filling with acrylics or wood. The area to be removed is outlined by a thin, U-tipped graver. A line following that outline is then engraved, 1–2mm inside the line, by a slightly thicker U-section graver. The metal inside the two inner lines is removed with the U-tipped graver and the line is flattened with a flat-bottomed engraver. The area left up to the first outline is removed with the first or second engraver, and a "spitstick" is used to neaten up the edges, but take care not to undercut the edge.

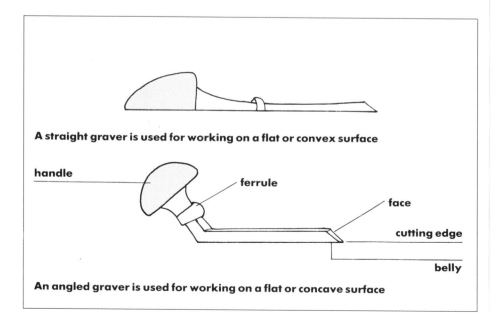

A straight graver is used for working on a flat or convex surface

handle
ferrule
face
cutting edge
belly

An angled graver is used for working on a flat or concave surface

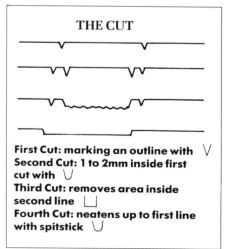

THE CUT

First Cut: marking an outline with ∨
Second Cut: 1 to 2mm inside first cut with ∪
Third Cut: removes area inside second line ⊔
Fourth Cut: neatens up to first line with spitstick ∪

Repoussé and Chasing

Repoussé and chasing work are usually done in conjunction. Repoussé is a relief pattern that is formed from the underside of the silver. Chasing is a means of marking, delineating and modelling from the top of the silver. The tools for both processes, which are very similar, should be kept clean and dry to prevent rust. The work must be supported in both instances, and this is usually done in a pitch bowl.

YOU WILL NEED

Pitch bowl and wooden ring
Selection of punches
Chasing hammer
Ball-pein hammer

You can buy sets of punches that will give you a selection of useful shapes and outlines. However, you can always make your own for a particular job or to create a few shapes that you know you will use. Use tool steel stock, cut and ground to shape as described in the section on texturing (see 41). Before you begin work, scribe the lines of your pattern onto the top side of the silver, allowing for an extra area of silver to be left all round. Place the work in the pitch by gently heating the pitch with your flame and laying the work in it while it is warm. Allow the pitch to just come up over the edges and, with wet fingers, build up the edges a little to give a good hold.

This bangle shows both repoussé and chasing techniques. Chris Morphy.

PUNCHES AND THEIR USES

Linear or tracer punch These are used on the front of work to make lines and curves. They are chisel-shaped and have a bevelled edge, which can vary in width. The lines of a tracer punch show through to the back, so they can be used as a guide for later repoussé work.

Linear or tracer punches

Modelling punch Used on the front of the work to define and shape the relief forms of repoussé, modelling punches come in various shapes – round, rectangular, oval, triangular and square.

Modelling punches

Matting punch Matting punches are also used on the front of your work, but they are mainly for making a background texture or patterned area. The heads of these punches are not polished because the pattern might become less defined.

Matting punches

Embossing punch Often used on the reverse of silver for raising ridges, curves and bumps. These punches also come in a variety of shapes – square, round and oval, for example, but they always have rather flat faces and rounded edges. They are highly polished.

Embossing punches

Planishing punch Planishing punches are used to smooth and burnish a raised surface. They have flat, smooth faces, which are highly polished. They can also be used for flattening areas of background.

Planishing punches

Hollow-faced punch These punches are used from either underneath or on top of the silver to create circular lines, which can be either raised or sunk. The faces are made by drilling out or shaping with a rotary burr on the pendant motor.

Hollow-faced punches

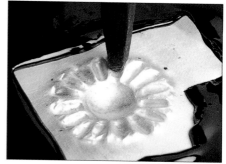

1 Hold your chasing punch at an angle and tilted away from you. Use a chasing hammer to tap the punch and let it move towards you. Hold the tool on one side with your first three fingers and, on the opposite side, with your thumb. Your little finger should touch the silver and guide your hand over the surface. Because only the corner of the punch does the chasing, by tilting it you can see what you are doing. Work from the inner part of your design to the outer and remember that you are not cutting a line, only making an indentation.

2 Repoussé punches are held vertically just above the silver and tapped rhythmically with a chasing hammer. For heavier work use a ball-pein hammer. Remember that you need to anneal your work as it becomes hard. Remove it from the pitch by gently playing a flame around the silver and then lifting up the corner with a pair of old pliers or tweezers. The pitch will burn off your work as you anneal it. All pitch should be removed before pickling, or it becomes hard and difficult to remove. Pitch can also be removed by immersion in turpentine.

3 After completing repoussé work it may be necessary to finish off the work from the front. Make sure that any raised areas made with the repoussé punches are supported at the back by running pitch into them before you replace the work in the pitch. Flat background decoration can be finished on a flat wooden or steel surface.

4 When you have completed all your surface decoration, pierce away the extra surrounding metal. You can now solder on fittings, set stones and so on, and polish.

A neckpiece set with tigerion. Chris Morphy.

Etching

Etching is the process of removing an exposed area of silver by means of an acid solution. It is often used in preparation for enamelling, for cold-casting acrylics and for general surface decoration. Those areas of work that are not to be etched are made safe by the application of a coat of stop-out varnish. The silver should be clean and free from grease.

YOU WILL NEED

Stop-out medium
Etching medium of 3 parts water to 1 part nitric acid mixed in a bowl

Stop-out is an acid-resistant medium which will stay on the silver as the acid eats away exposed areas. A variety of stop-outs or resists are available:

Beeswax Warm your cleaned metal and immerse it in molten beeswax. Remove and allow to cool before cutting your pattern through the wax with a scriber or craft knife. After etching, heat it all up to remove the wax. Any stubborn bits will come off with acetone.

Shellac You can either dip a whole piece into shellac and scribe through the design, or apply shellac with a paintbrush, leaving unpainted those areas to be etched.

Quick-dry stopping varnish Apply the varnish with a paintbrush or immerse your work in the varnish and scratch the design through. Leave to dry. Heat gently with a flame to dry it if necessary. If it is still wet when the work is immersed in the acid it will lift away.

When you use a stop-out, make sure that the reverse of the silver and all the sides are well coated. Any seepage here could be disastrous.

Etched silver earrings. Jenny Turtill.

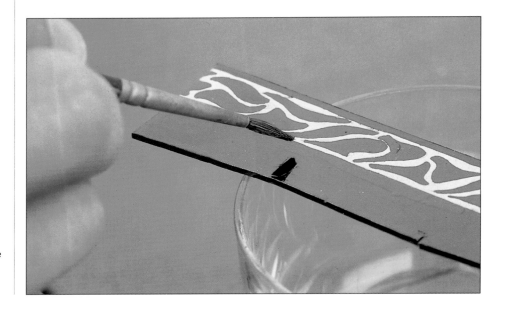

THE ETCHING MEDIUM

1 When the stop-out is completely dry, immerse your piece into the acid. After a few seconds you will see bubbles appearing on the exposed surface.

2 Use a feather to tickle these away and keep gently agitating the surrounding acid. Keep a close eye on the etching process to make sure it is under control. If you think it is etching too quickly, mix a weaker solution; if it is too slow, carefully add more acid.

3 Leave your work immersed until you can clearly feel the etched line – 0.5mm – with the tip of a scriber. About 30 minutes should be sufficient. As well as eating downwards, acid eats sideways, so very thin lines can be vulnerable. If you spot this happening, remove the work and renew the stop-out down

A feather is used to brush away bubbles which formed when the silver was etched.

The outline is pierced after stop out has been removed.

CAUTION
Nitric acid is dangerous. Wear rubber gloves throughout the process; **always** add acid to water **never** vice versa, and make sure you work in a well-ventilated place.

the edge. Generally, etching is best suited to soft curved lines.

4 Remove the stop-out by soaking in turpentine or heat your work gently to melt wax. Do not pierce out your outline until the etch is completed to allow for any possible leakage.

For etching on gold see Working with Gold (page 93). For etching copper, use a similar solution as for silver, or a half-and-half mixture of water and hydrochloric acid.

If you are making several articles to one design and a very accurate etch is needed, take your design and a suitable sheet of silver to a professional photo-etcher. The design is etched photographically across the silver to produce as many pieces as you want. Each one is then pierced out from the sheet, although it is possible to photo-etch from both back and front,

Silver earstuds etched and gold plated.
Jenny Turtill.

which, in effect, cuts right through the silver and eliminates the need for piercing. Unless you are making several items, photo-etching is not economical.

A slower etch using 8 parts water to 1 part nitric acid is particularly suitable for enamelling, because a slower etch is easier to control. It is important that the sides do not undercut for enamelling, so keep an eye on your piece during the etch. It will probably take up to 3 to 4 hours to etch down to 0.3–0.4mm.

Enamelling

Enamelling is the art of fusing glass to metal. The process imparts a whole new dimension to jewellery because it is possible to add so much varied colour. Work that is to be enamelled must be very carefully constructed because it has to undergo high temperatures in a kiln. You should try to set aside a special area in your workshop for enamelling, as far away from your polisher as possible. Apart from a kiln and the enamels themselves, you will not need much extra equipment.

YOU WILL NEED

Kiln
Assortment of transparent, opaque and translucent enamels
Cloisonné wire
Paintbrush
Dental tools
Paper clips
6mm wood dowelling
Palette for colours
Mortar and pestle
Glass brush
Stands for work
Wire mesh tray
Long fork
Etching equipment

The silver is cleaned with a glass brush under running water.

PREPARING THE SILVER

Pierce your design or make your shape on the silver, anneal, pickle and rinse. Silver needs to be very clean and free from grease for the enamel to adhere well, so wash it thoroughly under running water and brush the whole surface with a "glass brush". The water will then stay on the surface of the silver without running off to form little globules.

PREPARING ENAMELS

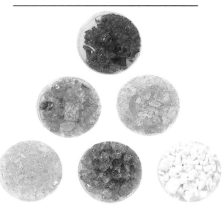

A selection of coloured transparent enamels in lump or "Frit" form, with an opaque white enamel.

1 Enamels are supplied in lump or powder form. Both need grinding and washing before they are placed into or onto the silver.

2 Place the enamel in the mortar and pestle, add water and grind until it is very fine. Swill away the water and add fresh water, which is swirled around and thrown away.

3 Repeat this process until the water is absolutely clear, then give the enamels a final rinse with distilled water. They are then ready for use.

4 Powdered enamels do not need so much grinding as they are already fairly fine, but the washing should be just as scrupulous. After grinding, keep the enamels under water to stop dust and dirt getting into them. Any dirt fired into enamel will show up as an ugly black mark.

Enamel laid directly onto silver leaving a fine border. Jinks McGrath.

This is the reverse of the piece on the left which is "counter enamelled". Jinks McGrath.

There are several different methods of enamelling, which depend on how the silver has been worked in order to receive the enamel.

The first method is simply to apply enamel directly onto the silver. It can be taken right up to the edge, or a little border of silver can be left. It should be counter enamelled, and depth of colour is added with every additional layer of enamel. It does not usually need stoning down.

COUNTER ENAMEL

Because enamel expands and contracts at a different rate from silver, it is often necessary to counter enamel the back of your piece to avoid chipping and cracking on the front. If a piece is not counter enamelled, it tends to bend backwards, although this can be helped by using a thicker-gauge silver. Counter enamelling can be done at the same time as the first firing as long as you support the work without anything touching the enamel.

CHAMPLEVÉ

In French this means "raised field", which is a good description of the process. The enamel is laid in etched-out or engraved-out areas of silver and "raised" or built up until it reaches the same height as the remaining silver. The enamel should be approximately 0.3– 0.5mm deep and less than half the full thickness of the silver. If the ground has been engraved out, the surface should be as smooth as possible, because different levels will result in different tones in the enamel. It is possible to achieve the same effect by soldering a pierced piece of silver, approximately 0.5mm, to a backing sheet approximately 0.75mm. You should use enamelling or hard solder, and if any solder flows into the area to be enamelled it must be removed with either a riffler file or a burr on the pendant motor.

Champlevé enamelled earrings. Jinks McGrath.

CLOISONNÉ

This French word means "partitioned" which again describes this method very well. Very thin silver or gold wires called cloisonné wires, are laid onto or into the silver to form a pattern or picture. The cells thus formed are filled with different coloured enamels. The wire, which is 0.2– 0.3mm thick, is flattened, bent to shape with pliers and exactly follows the lines of your design as they are laid onto the silver. Wires can be held on concave or convex surfaces with a special enamelling glue, which burns away in the kiln without leaving any marks. Before cloisonné wires are laid, the area should be enamelled with a clear or flux enamel, the wires laid on top and the piece refired. The wires will sink in far enough for them to be held in place, and any rogue wires can be pushed flat when it has cooled. The cells will need to be filled and fired four to five times with the coloured enamels until they reach the same height as the edges or the top of the cloisonné wire.

Cloisonné earstuds with gold border. Jinks McGrath.

BASSE TAILLE

Pattern engraved into silver earrings for basse taille enamel. Jinks McGrath.

The French phrase means "deep cut", and this technique can be used with champlevé or when you are enamelling straight onto the silver. The background silver is engraved or chased to show an outline or pattern beneath the transparent enamel. The colour of the enamel deepens as layers are built up, so when additional layers have to be laid into a carved pattern, the pattern will show as a darker-coloured area.

PLIQUÉ À JOUR

Pliqué à jour eardrops. Jinks McGrath.

This enamel resembles a stained glass window. The enamel is suspended between silver "walls" and is fired without any backing so that the light can shine through both sides. Silver for pliqué à jour can be pierced out of silver sheet, or a framework of wires can be built up and soldered to a thicker outer frame. The design should not include sharp-angled corners or large gaps; the enamel will not hold itself in cells larger than about 6mm square. Pliqué à jour enamel can be fired suspended on supports in the kiln, and until the cells are completely filled the enamel should remain slightly underfired. Alternatively, the silver can sit on a sheet of mica while it is filled with enamel. Pieces of the mica will fire into the enamel, but these can be stoned off before a final suspended firing. Pliqué à jour enamels are stoned down as other enamels, but remember that they are fairly fragile. Running water prevents particles of stone getting rubbed into the enamel, so make sure that all the rubbing down is done under a tap. The final firing should be rather shorter than the previous firings and a little hotter.

PAINTED ENAMELS

These are usually applied onto a slightly domed surface, which has been enamelled with hard white before painting. The very finely ground painting enamels, which do not need grinding and washing, are mixed to a workable paste with lavender oil or water on a flat glass sheet and applied with a brush. The picture is built up over many firings. Before firing, hold the work at the mouth of the kiln for about a minute to dry. Painted enamels should be watched carefully and usually fire quicker than other enamels.

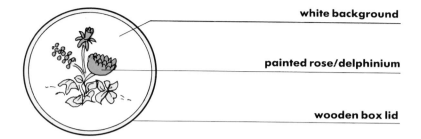

white background

painted rose/delphinium

wooden box lid

GRISAILLE

This technique is similar to painting enamels, but it uses only black and white. White enamel is fired onto a black background. As the white sinks into the black, more white is added to build up a picture full of tones, shadows and highlights.

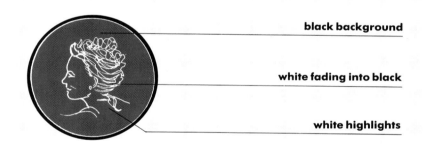

black background

white fading into black

white highlights

THE KILN

Most enamels will fuse at temperatures of 700–900°C (1300–1660°F). The kiln should be at temperature before you begin firing. If you have no temperature gauge on your kiln, a good red heat will generally be sufficient to fire painted enamels and possibly some reds. A cherry red will fire most fluxes, many transparent enamels and opaque and opalescent enamels. A bright orange, being very hot, will fire some hard transparent enamels and overfire others.

TEST PIECE

Always fire a test piece first. Use a piece of properly prepared silver, and try firing your selected colours at different temperatures. Watch to see how and when each one fires and, from the results, work out the order of firing the piece. It is a good idea to keep the results of each of your samples as a reference. Fire colours direct onto silver and on top of a clear flux, and onto silver and gold foil to assess whether you need to use flux on your piece.

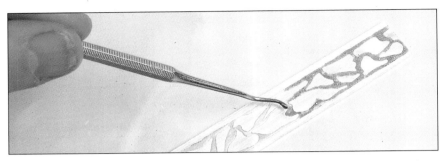

Wet packing ground enamel.

USING ENAMELS

After all your enamels are ground and washed, place them wet into a palette ready for use. Use either the end of a quill, a small spatula or a paintbrush to place a thin layer of flux or enamel on your piece. If necessary, draw away excess water with the edge of a clean tissue. This is helpful when you are laying one colour close up to another. Lay the enamel on a sheet of mica or use a support and place it on a steel mesh tray. Allow it to dry either on top of the kiln or nearby.

When it is dry, place the mesh tray on a long fork, and put it in the centre of the kiln. At first it will darken as the metal oxidizes, then the enamel will start to resemble orange peel, then suddenly shine. It can now be removed from the kiln and left to cool. If it is cooled too quickly it may crack. Repeat this process until the height of the enamel is the same as the cloisonné or the silver surrounds.

It is better to add five thin layers of enamel than two thick layers, because it is easy to trap air in thick enamel, which results in pits in the surface that can be difficult to fill. If this does happen, drill out the pit completely and fill the hole with two or three new layers of enamel. When enamel is overfired it looks rather mottled and develops black lines round the edge; transparent enamels can look dull and lifeless. This can sometimes be rectified by refiring at a lower heat, but overfiring and underfiring should be avoided by good testing methods.

FINISHING

When the enamel is just higher than the surface of the silver it should be ground down ready for finishing. Use a carborundum stone for grinding, and hold the work under a running tap and grind until the enamel is level. Any depressions can be filled up, fired and then reground. After the carborundum stone, use wet and dry papers to give a finer finish to both the enamel and the silver. Then refire the piece at a slightly higher temperature and for a shorter time to restore the shiny surface. Surfaces can be left matt by omitting the final firing. After the final firing the work can be polished as for silver, but some enamels absorb dark polish, so it is always wise to try the polish on the test piece to see if your enamel is suitable. Pumice paste will give an interesting finish to enamels. Silver will be oxidized after enamelling, and although it is usually possible to pickle the piece to get rid of it, some enamels are sensitive to acid, so once again experiment with a test piece first.

Unused enamel can be dried and stored in airtight containers for future use. However, old or badly dried enamel can cause problems, so I prefer to throw it all away when I have finished with it.

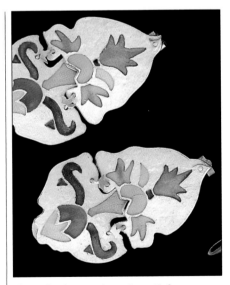

Champlevé enamel earrings. Jinks McGrath.

FINDINGS

I like to solder all findings on with hard or enamelling solder before enamelling. If you take care these will be safe in the kiln. Some enamellers prefer to solder after enamelling with easy solder either in the kiln or on a soldering block, but I find this method can cause cracking and discoloration. Experiment to see which way suits you.

Casting

There are times in jewellery making when several identical shapes need to be made or a three-dimensional piece is too difficult to model in silver. Workshop casting or commercial casting is used in these circumstances. Casting is the process of pouring molten silver into a prepared mould, cooling it and then refining and finishing the result. There are various ways of achieving this, each method depending on what the finished result is to be. In your workshop there are three ways of casting:

▮ Cuttlefish bone is simple but effective
▮ Drop casting is totally unpredictable but fun
▮ A centrifugal casting machine is very effective but represents a fairly large investment, and it needs space. This method is also known as cire perdue.

PREPARING A CUTTLEFISH MOULD

Cuttlefish bones, which can be bought from pet shops or picked up from a beach if you live near the sea, can be useful for casting a one-off piece in silver. Make your model from modelling wax, perspex, wood, brass or natural "found" objects or cut directly into the cuttlefish. The shape should be free from undercuts.

1 Using a piercing saw cut away a straight line across the top and bottom of the cuttlefish bone.

2 Carefully pierce down the middle of the bone. Place the pierced sides on a flat bed with dry emery paper and rub gently to make them perfectly flat.

3 Take your model and carefully push it into one half of the bone about one-third of the way down the side, with the heaviest part of the model nearest the bottom end of the bone. Push the model into the bone until just over half of it is embedded.

4 Place a piece of round copper wire, approximately 1mm round, at each corner – not too close to the edge – leaving about 10mm all round. Take the other half of the cuttlefish bone and gently press it down onto the locating pegs and onto the other half of the model. The two sides of the bone should fit closely together. Trim the sides and scribe location lines across the join.

5 Use a small hand drill to make a hole at the top so that it just meets the model. The diameter of the drill bit should be such that it leaves clearance of at least 6mm of cuttlefish bone.

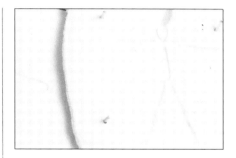

6 Gently prise the two sides apart, remove the model and scrape away a cone-shaped channel around both sides of the drill hole. Scribe two or three vent lines, leading away from the base of the indentation to allow gases to escape when casting.

7 Blow away any dust and replace the two halves together. Parcel it all together with binding wire.

CASTING INTO THE CUTTLEFISH

8 If you have made your model in perspex or wax you will need approximately 11 times its weight in silver for casting. Cut scrap pieces of silver into small pieces and place them in a crucible with some flux.

9 Position the cuttlefish bone with the hole in the top, supporting it so that it stays upright.

Molten silver is poured into the opening of the cuttlefish bone.

10 With a strong flame, melt the silver in the crucible, watch it become molten, when it will form a soft, runny ball, then, keeping the flame gently on it to keep it molten, pick up the crucible with tongs and pour the molten silver quickly and smoothly into the cuttlefish bone so that the silver does not solidify. Allow it to cool.

11 Unwrap the cuttlefish bone and remove the casting with tongs. Pickle and clean with files and finally polish.

DROP CASTING

1 Melt scraps of silver in a crucible and have a long flask of water, a bowl of ice or a tumbler of water close by.

2 As the silver melts, pour it into the water or onto the ice and watch as it forms interesting shapes. Some of the pieces will not be usable – they can always be melted again – but you may well be able to incorporate some of them into your designs.

Necklace with cuttlefish castings and haematite beads. Jenny Turtill.

CENTRIFUGAL CASTING

Selection of waxes used for model making.

If you do not have access to a centrifugal casting machine but would like to try this method, enrol in a special casting course.

All the models for this method are made in wax, which comes in sheets, small to large diameter rods, hard blocks of modelling wax (which are cut and filed in the same way as metal), long blocks and crude ring shapes. Electric wax-filled modelling pens are useful for edges and for forming flowing lines.

Once a model which can be undercut has been made, a wax "sprue" is attached, in such a way that the flowing molten silver does not have to go back on itself. The sprue is attached to the model at a thick rather than thin area, and the join should be nicely rounded with sprue wax. The sprue is then attached to a rubber base. A metal tube fits into the rim of the rubber base. The model should have space all around it and the top of the model should not reach as high as the rim of the metal tube. A wetting agent may be painted on the model at this point. An "investment", usually a powder similar to plaster of Paris, is mixed with water, which should weigh about 40 per cent of the weight of the investment powder to make a smooth investment. Mix the investment thoroughly and then pour it into the tube containing the model, taking care not to allow air bubbles to form around the model. The whole flask is then placed on a vibrating surface so that any air bubbles are forced to the surface. Commercial vibrators can be bought for this purpose, but you could make use of the vibrations of other machines such as a food mixer or washing machine. The investment is allowed to dry for about two hours. The flask is turned upside down and put in the kiln and heated to 650–750°C (1200–1380°F). This temperature is maintained for about 30 minutes, after which it can be lowered and held at about 450°C (850°F) for a further hour.

The flask is then removed from the kiln with special tongs and placed in the casting machine. Small pieces of silver, weighing about 11 times the weight of the wax model plus a bit more for the sprue, are melted in a charcoal crucible and placed in the casting machine. Some machines have a ceramic crucible, which has an open top, so the silver can be melted *in situ*. When the silver is molten, the spring on the machine is released, and, as the machine spins round, the molten silver flies into the burnt-out wax pattern in the flask opposite. The flask can then be removed and plunged into a bucket full of water and the casting retrieved and revealed! It is then filed, cleaned and polished.

Modelling wax is cut with a piercing saw.

Modelling wax is filed into shape.

The top of this modelling wax has been passed through a low flame, which gives a smooth, almost watery look to it.

COMMERCIAL CASTING
RUBBER MOULD INJECTION

For this method of casting the model is usually made from silver. It is finished to a very high quality to ensure a good casting and fitted with a metal sprue. The model is then sent to commercial casters. If you are unsure about the best position for the sprue, ask the casters to place it for you. The casters make a rubber mould around your model, which is then cut in half and the model removed. When the mould is fitted together again, hot wax is injected into it, and in this way as many identical wax models as you need can be made. The wax models are next sprued onto a "tree", which is placed in investment and the lost-wax casting technique is employed. The castings will be returned to you, although the rubber mould is usually retained by the casters for further castings. You will have to clean, file, polish and assemble the castings, which can be soldered as normal. Unfortunately, because of

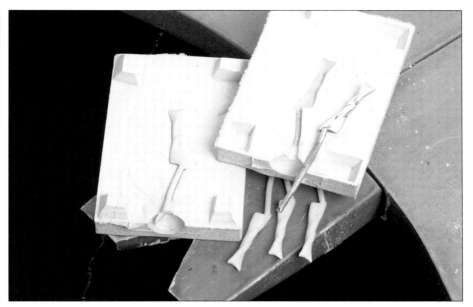

The rubber mould is formed around your original model and sprue. Here it is in two halves with some wax models, which have been injected into the cavity before being sprued up again and made ready for placing in the investment.

the high temperatures involved, castings are usually marked with fire stain, but this can be dealt with in any of the ways described in the section on annealing and soldering (see page 32).

Occasionally a casting will have a deep pock mark. It is impossible to fill such marks neatly because of the porosity of casting, and it is best to scrap such castings. A reputable casting firm should not supply too many of these.

Cast silver necklace. Jinks McGrath.

Cast silver necklace. Jinks McGrath.

SETTING FACETED STONES

FACETED STONES

For setting purposes, a faceted stone has three important parts — the table, the girdle and the culet. There are several different ways in which faceted stones can be successfully mounted.

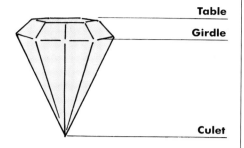

Table
Girdle
Culet

USING ROUND WIRE

1 Make a small domed back plate as before, and solder to it a round wire peg that will fit the pearl or bead. Solder the back of the plate to your piece of jewellery, or solder an earring pin to the back of the plate.

2 Use a fine saw blade to cut about halfway down the pin, and use a file to make a small, tapered wedge that will fit into the saw cut. Push the wedge into the top of the wire and push the peg into the pearl or bead, tapping it in place very gently. You can use cement if you wish, but this may not be necessary.

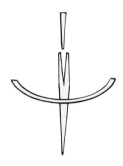

Pearl beads cemented onto twisted square wire.

FLUSH SETTING

1 Drill a hole through the silver; the hole should be about 2mm smaller than the diameter of the stone.

2 Use the pendant motor with a burr attachment to remove enough silver for the stone to sit in the hole. Alternatively, you could use a small hand drill.

3 File away the silver around the top edge of the bezel.

4 Sit the stone in the setting and burnish the bezel onto the stone.

5 Polish and finish.

SETTING IN TUBE OR CHENIER

Use chenier that has the same diameter as your stone or a fractionally larger diameter.

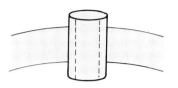

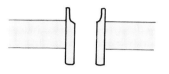

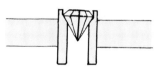

1 Drill a hole in your work that is exactly the same size as the chenier.

2 Solder the chenier into place, leaving the top proud so that the girdle of the stone will appear to sit on the top edge of the ring.

3 Use the pendant motor with a burr attachment or a small hand drill to remove the inside of the chenier to fit the stone as far as the top edge of your work.

4 Gently file around the top outer edge of the chenier.

5 Sit the stone in the tube and burnish the edges of the tube over the stone.

6 Polish and finish.

RUB-OVER SETTING FOR FACETED STONES

The faceted stone is fitted into the rub-over setting.

The setting is adjusted with burr in the pendant motor.

A pusher is used to rub the bezel onto the stone.

MAKING A COLLET USING CHENIER

1 Choose chenier that has an outside diameter slightly greater than that of your stone and fix it to your stick with melted setter's wax or jeweller's wax.

2 Use the pendant motor with a burr attachment to remove the inside edge of the silver down as far as the level of the girdle of the stone.

3 Use a fine blade in a piercing saw to cut away the chenier, leaving the number of prongs necessary to hold the stone. Hold the saw at an angle to avoid marking the prongs.

4 File the saw cuts to give smooth, bevelled edges.

5 Turn the collet over and use a file to make notches in the base to allow as much light as possible to reach the stone. Solder the collet to your work.

6 Use a file to make a notch in the top edge to hold the girdle.

7 Sit the stone in the collet and push down the prongs to hold it securely in position.

MAKING A COLLET USING WIRE

1 Measure the diameter of the stone at a point slightly below the girdle and at a point just above the culet.

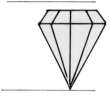

2 Make two rings of the diameters above out of approximately 0.75mm wire. If your stone is large, use heavier gauge wire.

3 Cut two pieces of wire that are longer than the height of the stone. Solder the wire together by filing a notch in the centre of each length and placing them at right angles, one on top of the other.

4 Solder the smaller wire ring centrally under the wire cross, with the larger ring on top. Pierce away the wire of the cross pieces at the points where they cross the smaller, lower ring.

5 Measure the point where the girdle of the stone will lie on the wires and use a triangular file to make a groove. Bend the wires upwards.

6 Solder the collet to your work and use a needle file to neaten the edges of the wire.

7 Sit the stone in the collet and use a burnisher to rub the wires over the stone.

This basic technique can be applied to any shape of stone by altering the shape of the rings — to fit an oval, for example — and by increasing the number of wires or claws.

MAKING A COLLET USING SHEET SILVER

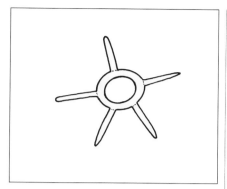

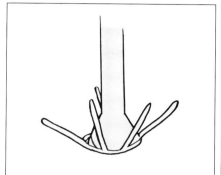

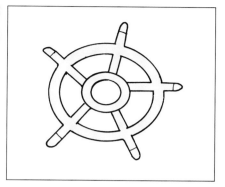

1 Pierce out a suitable shape for an oval or round stone.

2 File a small groove where the girdle of the stone will fit.

3 Place the collet on the pitch and gently hit a doming punch held in the centre, which will allow the claws to come up.

4 Solder to your piece.

5 Sit in the stone and turn over the claws.

SETTING A STONE IN A CLAW SETTING

Setting a stone in a claw setting. The claws are adjusted for the stone and then pushed down onto the stone. The excess length is clipped off with side cutters and then burnished to a thumb nail finish.

SQUARE AND RECTANGULAR RUB-OVER SETTING

1 Measure each side of the stone and mark the length of each side on a strip of silver that is the appropriate thickness for the setting, adding twice the thickness of the silver to each measurement.

2 A soldered join is best halfway down one of the longer sides. Mark the position accordingly.

3 Use a three-corner file to remove just more than half the thickness of silver at each corner mark.

4 Bend up with flat-nose pliers and solder, running solder up each corner at the same time.

5 Either solder onto a backing sheet and pierce out the centre, or solder in a bearer wire.

6 Set the stone with a small punch, clean the edges and burnish.

TAPERED RECTANGULAR OR SQUARE SETTING

1 Use 1.5mm silver sheet and measure the width of the stone at the girdle and 1.5mm below the girdle.

2 Mark on the silver the outline of the girdle and then mark the lower outline.

3 Pierce out from the inner line to the outer by leaning your saw between the two lines as you cut.

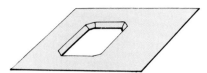

4 Mark an edge 1–1.5mm away from the outer cut edge and pierce, using the same technique with the saw. Alternatively, pierce out the shape straight and file the taper.

5 Cut claws out of the same sheet and file a groove so that they fit each corner.

6 Solder the setting and claws to a base and then pierce away the inside at a similar angle so that the stone sits comfortably.

7 Before setting the stone, file the top edge of the claws to make a neat rub-over setting.

CONED COLLETS

Claw and rub-over settings sometimes need to be cone shaped. This shape can be cut from sheet or made by bending rectangular wire.

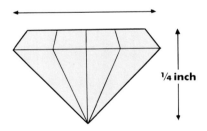

¼ inch

1 Take, for example, a faceted stone with a girdle diameter of 9mm. Find the circumference:

$$2 \times \frac{22}{7} \times 4.5 = 28.28mm$$

Allow an extra 2mm length for the claws.

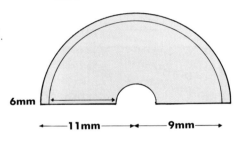

6mm

11mm — 9mm

2 Draw a semicircle with a 9mm radius, then draw another semicircle, adding 2mm to allow for the claws.

3 Measure the length of stone from the girdle to the culet – 6mm – and draw another semicircle, 6mm below the first.

4 Pierce out a strip of silver that is this shape, and bend it up with round or half-round pliers. Solder.

5 Fasten the collet onto the stick with sealing wax, file or pierce out the claws and file a groove in the claws for the girdle of the stone (as for chenier).

6 Turn the collet over and file out notches in the bottom.

7 Solder onto the work. These collets can be used for rectangular and square stones. Mark out the length of each side within the correct circumference line. Make grooves with a three-corner file where the strip bends. Bend up with flat-nose pliers and solder, flushing solder into all the corners.

PAVE SETTINGS

Stones are sometimes set in clusters or in a line very close to each other, a method known as pave setting. This can be done by using your piercing saw to make the shape required for the stone to sit in. To make a setting for a straight strip:

1 Drill holes smaller than the width of the girdle of the stones through the work in such a position that the stones will sit almost touching each other.

2 Scribe the width of the girdles on the silver outside the drill holes.

3 Hold the piercing saw at an angle through the hole and gently stroke the blade up to the scribed line. Cut without opening out the drilled hole at the bottom.

4 If necessary, you can open out the bottom by turning the silver over and using your saw in the same way, taking care not to open out the diameter of the drilled hole.

RAISING GRAINS

For pave settings the silver at the edge of the stones is raised by means of a graver. It can be raised either all the way round or just at opposite corners, which are then formed into little balls that are pushed over to hold the stone in place. This is called raising grains.

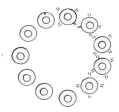

1 Place a half-round scorper about 1mm from the edge of the stone and dig into the metal, pushing down and forwards.

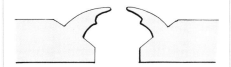

2 Lift the scorper to raise the sliver of silver over the stone. Repeat this action twice more, from the same starting place, but the second time push the scorper to the right and work it up, and the third time push it to the left. Repeat this process at opposite corners.

3 The balls are formed with a beading tool, which encloses the turned up slivers into its concave head. If you make a side to side movement and, at the same time, push downwards, the little silver balls will form over the stone.

4 Alternatively, drill holes at each corner and solder wires, which fit snugly into them, in position to form little claws.

A pave setting. The holes are prepared to receive the stones with the drill on the pendant motor and then set in.

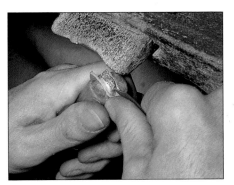

A half-round scorper is used to raise the grains round each diamond, and then the grains are pushed down with the beading tool.

The area around the grains is cleaned and the edges cleaned with the spitstick.

1

2

3

1 Silver mask necklace
with carnelian Chinese
turquoise beads. Alan
Vallis.

2 Cast silver necklace.
Alan Vallis.

3 Reticulated silver
necklace and stones.
Ruta Brown.

4

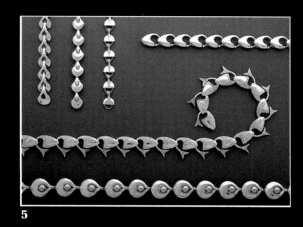

5

4 **Silver brooch with fine gold decoration set with pink and green tourmaline. Pat McAnally.**

5 **Silver and gold necklaces. Brett Payne.**

6 **Silver brooch with fine gold decoration set with lapis lazuli. Pat McAnally.**

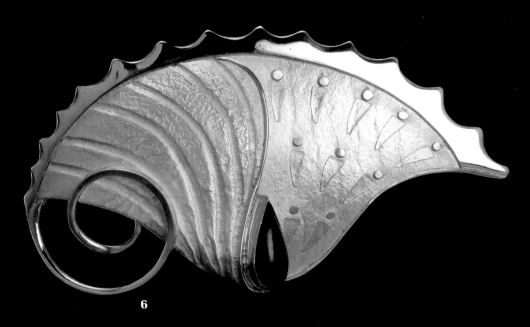

6

More Joints

There are many other ways, in addition to soldering, of attaching one piece of silver to another. Work out what kind of joint is needed for your piece – a necklace requires a different movement from a bracelet, and a joint for one may not be appropriate for another. The simplest way of joining two units is by means of a jump ring, but although jump rings work well they do not always look good, so it is worth exploring other, interesting ways of joining.

An unusual fastening makes the back of this necklace more interesting. Alexandra Coppen.

OVERLAPPING UNIT

1 Drill two holes in each unit where the join is to be.

2 Solder a length of wire in one hole. Slot the second unit over the wire.

3 Take a small jump ring, which just fits over the wire, and place the ring 1–2mm above the units.

4 Solder the ring to the wire.

5 Remove the excess wire and file smooth.

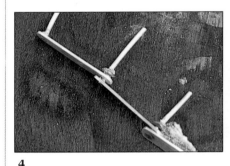

4

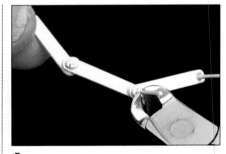

5

Silver and gold necklace with overlapping joints. Jinks McGrath.

HINGE

Chenier that is used for hinges has a slightly thicker wall than other chenier.

1 Choose chenier of a diameter which will be suitable for the hinge.

2 File a groove, to hold the chenier, along both ends of the silver to be hinged.

3 Hold the chenier in a jointing tool and cut off exactly the correct length – that is, the length of the whole hinge.

4 Mark on the surface of one side of the silver the point at which the two outer parts of the chenier will sit.

Lay the chenier on the silver and mark the chenier similarly.

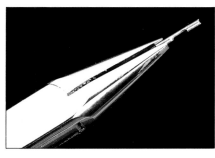

5 File away half the chenier between the two markings.

6 Lay the chenier along the silver with the filed side down and flux the two ends. Place a small paillon at either end and solder.

7 Cut away the remains of the middle section with a piercing saw.

8 Mark the other end of the silver where the middle section will be.

9 Cut the chenier to length.

10 Solder on the section using a small paillon.

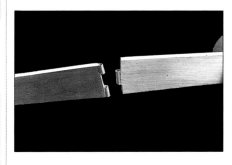

11 Check the alignment. Rivet a pin through the joint.

DIFFERENT JOINTS

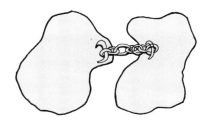

Hard solder balls onto both ends of wire or rod and place inside one half of a unit. Easy solder the other half on top.

Run a ball up a wire. Slot and bend the wire through both units and run a ball down the protruding wire.

Solder links onto the back of units and use chain or wire to link them.

Spread one end of round wire by forging, thread through two units and forge out the other end.

Another way of fastening a necklace. Use wire about 2.3mm in diameter and decorate the ends with fine wire rings.

BOX CATCH

The spring fitting (a) on a box catch (b) has to squeeze together while it is being slotted into the opening (c). The edge (d) fits behind the edge (e). By means of the top (f) you can push down (a) to release the catch.

Cut a silver shape (l) to fit your measurements. Pierce out shape (g) so that it is wide enough to take the two thicknesses of the spring fitting (a). Pierce out (i) to fit the tag (f). File along the lines of the box (l), fold up and flush solder into the corners. Fold over lid and solder all together. Cut out the spring fitting (a) from a sheet of silver, which should be long enough when folded for the end to go back beyond the tag (f) so that it can be soldered or joined to the other side of the work. If possible, solder (a) to the work before bending up so that you can harden the silver while it is still flat by tapping it on the anvil with your hammer; take care not to spread the silver when you do this. File out any marks. Fold up the spring fitting (a) and curl over the tag (f). Solder the box (l) to the other side of your work.

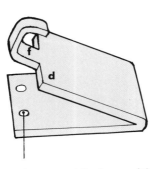

Allow enough space at the base of the spring in which to drill holes for slotting jump rings through or to pierce the shape of open rings.

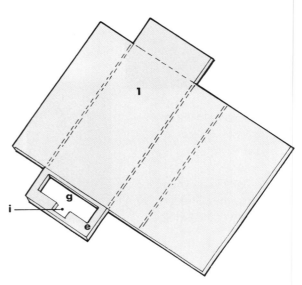

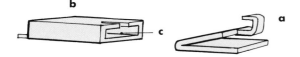

Cut along heavy lines, scribe, file and fold along dotted lines and solder to fit where the corners meet. File away at an angle of 45° for a good fit.

SPRING PIN

Solder chenier to either side of the work as for a hinge.

1 Take some D-section wire which will fit the inside diameter of the chenier and cut two lengths of the D-section, one slightly longer than the joint and the other long enough to turn a loop at the top.

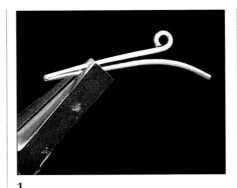

1

2 Solder the tips of the two ends together.

3 Harden the join by rolling it on the anvil and tapping it continuously with a small hammer. File it to fit if necessary.

4 Attach a chain to the pin through the loop and to the last section of the work.

Working with Gold

Gold is a beautiful metal to work with. It has a special quality and really comes alive as it is bent, stretched and moulded into shape. Golds above 14 carat are both malleable and resiliant, and the quality of colour makes them unsurpassable.

Pure gold, like pure silver, is generally too soft to use for any practical purpose in jewellery, and in order to make gold more workable other metals are alloyed with it. The proportions of these other metals determine the carat, the colour, the melting point and the hardness of gold. Pure gold is 24 carat. Other workable golds are 22 carat, 18 carat, 14 carat and, in Britain, 9 carat.

Silver locket with gold inlay. Jinks McGrath.

Assorted cufflinks set in 18 carat yellow gold. Gerald Benny.

Gold can be:
▌ Yellow – alloyed with silver/copper/zinc
▌ Green – alloyed with silver/copper
▌ White – alloyed with silver/platinum/palladium/nickel/zinc
▌ Red – alloyed with copper.

24 carat	
22 carat	
18 carat	Platinum Silver Copper Other metals
14 carat	
10 carat	Copper Silver Zinc Nickel
9 carat	

1

In general, yellow gold is the easiest to work. White gold, if it is not kept properly annealed while it is being worked, tends to become brittle. Green gold is usually fairly soft, and red gold needs to be kept reasonably soft for working. Gold of 10 carat and below is less malleable and does not have such good colour quality as higher carats. Store different carat golds separately, and when you are ordering gold ask the suppliers for their technical information sheets, which will give all the information about each type of gold – the melting, annealing and soldering temperatures, for example, and also the correct time to quench each one, and the best fluxes to use. Because gold has a high specific gravity – 19.3 per cent, compared with pure silver with a specific gravity of 10.56 per cent – an article in gold will weigh more than the same article in silver. The higher the carat, the more it will weigh.

1 Gold bracelet with emerald, amethyst and topaz. Simon Benny.

2 Handmade chain in 18 carat gold with diamonds. Alexandra Coppen.

2

ANNEALING

Yellow and green golds should be heated to a dull red and either quenched hot or allowed to air cool. Red gold is also heated to a dull red, but it is quenched while it is hot to avoid hardening. White gold is heated to a cherry red – a little higher than the others – but is left to cool for a while before quenching, or it can be left to air cool.

FLUXING

A flux of borax will sometimes burn out before gold solder flows, and more suitable fluxes, with a longer life at high temperatures, are used for gold. These are available in powder form and are mixed with water to form a creamy paste. Gold joins are fluxed in the same way as silver.

1

SOLDERING

Gold solders are bought in small, thin rectangles, which are printed with the carat and whether they are hard, medium or easy. The same carat and colour solder should be used as the carat and colour of the gold. Work through the solders as for silver. When you are soldering gold the areas to be joined should be clean, grease free and exactly lined up. Gold solder does not run in the same way as silver, and only very small paillons should be used. As it flows it looks shiny, like silver solder, but it will only spread, not run as silver does. After soldering, check with an eye glass to see if the gap is completely filled. If it is not, add a tiny sliver of gold and solder again. Gold can be soldered in just the area that needs to be joined, unlike silver which needs to be heated all through before the solder will flow. However, take care with the flame while soldering because gold gives little if no colour warning when it is getting too hot.

PICKLING

Gold can be pickled in the same sulphuric acid solution as silver, although it can pick up a rather silvery hue. A separate pickle of 8 parts water to 1 part nitric acid can be used for gold.

DANGERS

Take great care not to leave any deposits of lead, brass or aluminium on gold work. Avoid using a file or saw blade which has been used on these metals, and make sure that punches and hammer heads are clean before you use them on gold. If they are heated together with gold, deposits of these metals will collapse and burn holes in the surface of the gold – a calamity!

1 **Gold and silver brooch.
Pat McAnally.**

PIERCING AND FILING

Gold can be pierced and filed in much the same way as silver, although the blade tends to glide through 18 carat yellow! Save all the filings and off-cuts, however small, and keep different carat scrap separate.

Because gold is such an expensive metal it is worth making sure you know exactly how a piece of jewellery is to be made before you begin work. Practise any bending with copper or silver first, and if necessary make a jig, to ensure that the first bend of the gold is the right one. When you are making a larger piece, remember that gold weighs more than silver so ensure that your proposed size is appropriate. Plan pieces that are heavily contoured so that they can be cast – it will be less expensive and there will be less waste.

ENAMELLING

Most dealers supply special gold alloys for enamelling in 18 carat, 14 carat and occasionally in 9 carat. However, the best gold to use for enamelling is 24 carat (very soft) or yellow 18 carat. It is possible to enamel 24 carat and set it into an 18 carat setting. Transparent enamels look wonderful over gold, and reds and oranges need no undercoat flux. Also, many of the problems that occur with silver, disappear with gold. Gold foil is also used extensively in enamelling. The foil is 23.5 carat and gives a wonderful base for transparent colours. Foil is kept between two sheets of paper. To cut foil to fit a pattern, draw the outline on the paper and cut through all three layers with scissors or a craft knife. Lift the foil with tweezers or a paintbrush with a dab of enamelling and position it on the base coat of the enamel. Use a fine pin to prick little holes in the foil so that air bubbles are not trapped, and fire it into place. Enamel over the top.

ETCHING

To etch gold of 18 carats and lower, use either one of the following solutions:

Hydrochloric acid	8 parts		Nitric acid	1 part
Nitric acid	4 parts	OR	Hydrochloric acid	3 parts
Iron perchloride	1 part		Water	40/50 parts
Water	40/50 parts			

18 carat gold locket made from red, white and yellow golds and set with a diamond. Jinks McGrath.

SETTING STONES

Collets and bezels can generally be thinner than their silver counterparts. White 18 carat gold is often used for setting precious stones because it remains hard even if it is thin. Avoid using gold which is too thick for the setting, because it will be hard to coax down onto the stone.

GALLERY Gold

1 Gold buttons with
   enamelled centres.
   Gerald Benny.
2 Gold necklace set with
   diamonds and opal.
   Gerald Benny.

1

2

3

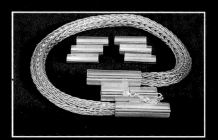

4

3 White, yellow and red
   18 carat gold set with
   sapphire. Jinks
   McGrath.
4 "Loop-in-Loop" gold
   and silver bracelet
   and earstuds.
   Alexandra Coppen.

PROJECT Hair Ornament

This piece involves doming, shaping, piercing and simulated forging. I used 0.75mm silver sheet for the main piece so that it is light enough to stay in place but heavy enough not to bend when it is in use.

YOU WILL NEED

Silver sheet 0.75 × 90 × 50mm
Scriber
Templates
Hammers and a wooden mallet
Lead blocks or a sandbag
Metal doming stakes
Needle files
Wet and dry papers
Polish
1 piece of silver approximately
    1.5 × 30 × 15mm
Flux and solder
Binding wire
Vice
Files
Drill
Silver wire 2.5 × 90mm
Anvil or steel plate

1 Draw or scribe the outside outline of the hair piece on to your silver sheet and pierce out.

2 Anneal, quench and dry.

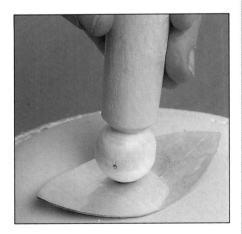

3 Use a wooden hammer to shape the piece on a sandbag or lead block.

4 Dome the piece all round by placing it on a metal stake and shaping it downwards all round with a wooden mallet.

5 Transfer the design to the shaped piece and pierce it out from the inside. I deliberately left the piercing of the pattern until after the piece was domed. If you try to dome, shape or bend after piercing, the corners will bend differently and the edges will tend to rise.

6 Clean all edges with needle files and wet and dry papers.

7 Use an oval needle file to flatten the entrance and exit areas to make them ready to accept the pin.

8 Polish and finish.

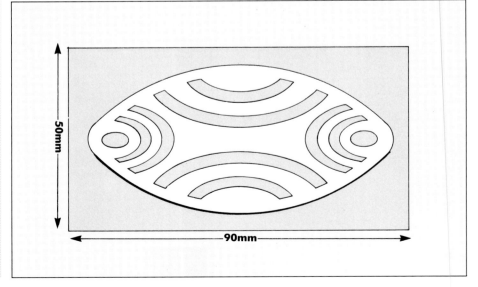

MAKING THE PIN

1 Take the piece of silver and place flux and paillons of hard solder over the top. Run the solder on it.

2 Quench, rinse and dry.

3 Quickly file the solder flat and cut the piece in half.

4 Flux the soldered sides, place them together and hold in place with binding wire. Place a little hard solder round the outside edges.

5 Solder it all together. Quench and dry.

6 File one edge straight.

7 Hold the piece in the vice and drill a hole in the centre of the straight edge, beginning with a 1mm drill bit and finishing with a drill that just allows the 2.5mm wire to fit snugly in.

8 Use easy solder to solder the wire into the silver head.

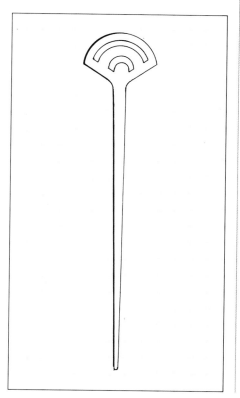

1

5

7

9 Forge out the silver head on the anvil or steel plate, using a heavy flat-faced hammer. Continue until it is large enough for the pattern to fit and until it is about the same thickness as the pin. It will need annealing during forging.

10 Now transfer the pattern to the head. Pierce out the inside areas first and finally the outline. File both sides smooth.

11 Shape the pin by filing and then hammering it to a point. The pin should be rolled along the anvil while you gently hammer to harden it.

12 File the edges, clean the whole pin with wet and dry papers and finally polish.

I gave the finished piece a matt finish by using a stainless steel mop on the polisher and then highlighted the edges with a polished burnisher.

PROJECT Necklace

This necklace uses a combination of silver, gold, copper, lapis lazuli, pearls and turned wooden discs. It is hung on tiger tail, which I recommend for hanging heavier pieces like this one. If you prefer not to use wood, look in your local bead shop or haberdasher's for suitable alternatives or make some painted wood or papier mâché ones yourself.

YOU WILL NEED

- Silver chenier 300mm long and with an outside diameter of 2.5–3mm
- Pitch, beeswax or fine sand; or fine wire
- Hammers and mallet
- Templates
- Jointing tool
- Files
- Polish
- Silver sheet 0.5 × 45 × 40mm
- Copper sheet 0.5 × 35 × 35mm
- Doming blocks
- Gold round wire approximately 60 × 1.5mm
- Silver round wire approximately 50 × 1.5mm
- Copper round wire approximately 40 × 1.5mm
- Rolling mill or anvil
- Flux and solder
- Drill
- Charcoal block
- Jump rings
- 1m tiger tail (very strong thread)
- Silver chenier 10mm long and with an outside diameter of 1.5mm
- Wooden discs or beads
- 8 lapis lazuli beads approximately 3mm across
- 8 pearls approximately 3mm across
- Pliers

BENDING THE CHENIER

1 Anneal the full length of the chenier. Quench, rinse and dry.

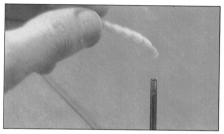

I used beeswax to fill up the chenier. A small flame keeps the chenier warm and gently lets the molten beeswax fill up the tube.

2 Plug one end of the chenier and fill it with heated pitch, melted beeswax or fine sand. Alternatively, coat with beeswax a length of wire that is longer than and has a smaller diameter than the chenier and insert it in the chenier.

3 Gently bend the chenier. Begin with a curve that is tighter than you need and take the curve right to the ends. Gently tap it to the right shape with a wooden mallet. Do not try to bend chenier unless you have filled up the interior: the inside curve will crumple and the outside will form

into kinks. Fine chenier, with a diameter of less than 1.5mm, could be bent carefully without filling. If you are making a gentle curve, use wire for the inside support.

4 Remove the beeswax or pitch by heating it gently. Remove the sand or wire.

5 Use a jointing tool to cut the chenier into four equal lengths. File away any rough edges and polish if you want a shiny finish.

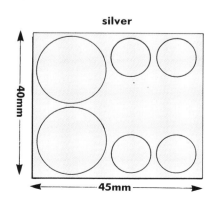

silver

40mm
45mm

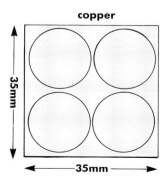

copper

35mm
35mm

MAKING THE SPHERES

I made the largest sphere of silver and gold, the middle two from copper and silver, and the two small ones from silver and copper. They are all made in the same way, so use the combination of your choice.

1 Texture the surfaces of the metals if required.

2 Cut two silver circles with diameters of 18mm, four copper circles with diameters of 16mm and four silver circles with diameters of 10mm.

3 Anneal, rinse and dry all the circles.

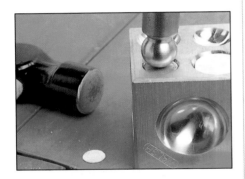

4 Dome each one until the largest are approximately 16mm in diameter, the middle are about 14mm in diameter and the smallest are about 8mm in diameter.

5 Flatten the top and bottom of the gold, silver and copper wire pieces by passing them through a rolling mill or gently hammering on your anvil.

6 Anneal the wire lengths, quench, rinse and dry.

7 Form circles with each length of wire so that one side of each sphere can sit on it without any gaps. Use the circumference of the domed spheres to calculate the length of wire needed for the rings. You will need to make them a little smaller to ensure a good fit.

8 Solder the rings with hard solder. Place a domed sphere on each ring, flux and, using hard solder again, place paillons on the outside edge. Solder up.

9 Drill a hole approximately 1mm across in the centre of the soldered dome.

10 Scrape out an area in your charcoal block for the soldered dome to sit in and place the other

half of the sphere onto the ring. Flux and place paillons of easy solder around the join and solder.

11 Drill a hole in the centre of this side.

12 File away excess metal from the centre of the spheres.

13 Clean and polish the spheres. Take care after quenching the spheres that you remove all the acid before working on them further. Boil them in a solution of soda crystals and water, rinse and let them sit on absorbent paper to make sure they are thoroughly dry.

14 Now solder two jump rings, attaching an S fastener to one of them.

WOODEN DISCS

The wooden discs I used are African blackwood and boxwood. They were turned and faced on a lathe and sanded. A hole was drilled in the centre. The edges are highlighted with a little linseed oil.

1 Thread the soldered jump ring with the fastener onto the length of tiger tail, followed by a pearl and lastly by a 5mm length of the small chenier.

2 Make a loop in the tiger tail and push the short end back through the pearl and chenier.

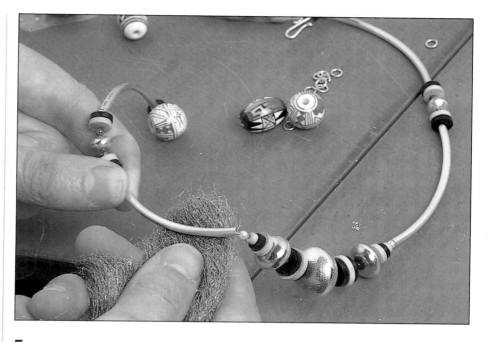

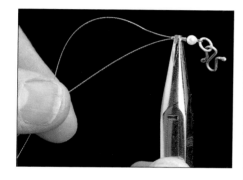

3 Squeeze the chenier together with serrated pliers.

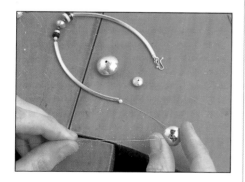

4 Thread on the larger chenier, followed by the pearls, wood, lapis, sphere, lapis, wood and pearl, or use whatever sequence you have chosen.

5 Continue threading until everything is on your necklace, finishing with the other 5mm piece of chenier, a pearl and the jump ring.

6 Thread the tiger tail back through the pearl and chenier, pull it all tight and squeeze the chenier together.

I finished the silver chenier by rubbing with fine steel wool along each length. If a polished finish is required, it is best to polish the silver before assembly.

7 Tuck the remaining tiger tail through the necklace.

PROJECT Enamelled Necklace

This project involves commercial casting and enamelling. If you do not have enamelling equipment you could either etch out the pattern or solder wires in position to form the picture and then oxidize the background.

YOU WILL NEED

Silver wire approximately
    4 × 30mm
Files
Templates
Pendant motor (optional)
Vice
Flux and solder
Files
Polish
Silver wire approximately
    0.75 × 500mm
Jump rings
Burnisher
Stop-out varnish or beeswax
Etching acid
Glass brush
Enamels: transparent blue flux,
    transparent golden brown,
    transparent rich pink,
    transparent walnut, transparent
    crystal blue, opaque white
Roll of 0.3mm cloisonné wire, 1m
    flattened in a rolling mill
Carborundum stone
Wet and dry papers
Kiln
Silver sheet 80 × 80 × 1.3mm –
    for enamelling
Wire mesh tray

MAKING THE CHAIN

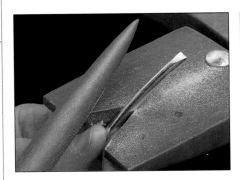

1 File the thick silver wire into a suitable shape for model link. Use a pendant motor to remove the excess silver if necessary, and anneal the piece to spread the ends by forging if you wish.

2 Hold one end in the safe jaws of a vice and twist through 360°.

3 Solder on a sprue and polish. Send your model to the casters, specifying how many pieces you require and allowing for one or two extras. It is possible to incorporate the wire ends on the model for casting. However, these ends are vulnerable to the casting process and can be easily broken. Because the ends are more delicate than the cast shapes, I prefer to solder on the wire ends.

4 When the pieces are ready, pierce away the remains of the sprue, file and clean each one.

5 Bend pieces of 0.75mm wire into shape to fit each casting, and use hard solder to solder one end to each section.

6 Leave the castings to air cool before cleaning in acid.

7 Turn each piece upside down and solder the wires onto the other ends with medium or easy solder. For a secure join, run some solder onto the wire ends as well as placing paillons on the casting.

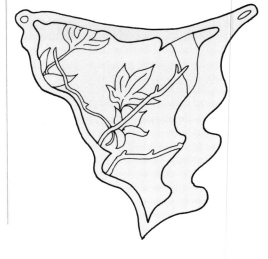

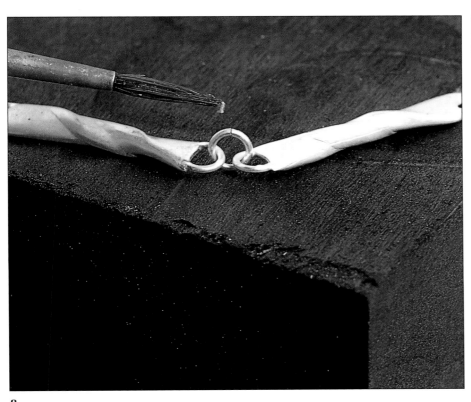

8

8 Solder the chain together with jump rings and easy solder, isolating each link before soldering.

9 Make a strong fastener for the chain out of slightly squared wire, tapered at each end and twisted in the middle. Bend it into an S shape and solder it to the last link.

10 Clean and finish each link, burnishing the high spots.

ETCHING THE CENTREPIECE

1 Transfer the outline of the *inside* of the centrepiece to your silver.

2 Paint up to the line and all over the silver with stop-out varnish or cover it with beeswax, taking care to cover all the edges. Wait for the front to dry before turning it over and covering the back in the same way. Use a wire support for this. If you do not want to enamel, paint stop-out varnish over the areas you do not wish to be etched to form the picture.

3 Immerse in a solution of nitric acid. I used 8 parts water to 1 part acid for a slow etch. Tickle with a feather from time to time. It took between 3 and 4 hours.

4 When you have etched away to a depth of about 0.3mm remove the piece from the acid, rinse in water and wash with turpentine to remove the stop-out varnish. Beeswax may be removed by gentle heat.

2

5 Pierce out the final shape of the piece and file the edges. Make a long gentle slope on the thick side of the silver.

6 Clean thoroughly under running water with a glass brush and leave in water until ready for use.

THE ENAMELLING

1 First do a test piece as described on page 75, using all the colours on top of the transparent flux. Take a note of any differences in firing temperature, and test in acid after firing. Test to see if any polish residue remains on the enamels after polishing.

2 Wash the enamels, then grind them until they are fine and place them one at a time into the palette.

3 Cover the whole of the etched-away area of the centrepiece with a thin layer of transparent blue flux.

4 Place your work on the wire mesh tray and leave to dry. You can help it to dry by putting the corner of a piece of absorbent paper just to the edge and drawing the water from the enamel.

5 Fire at about 800°C (1500°F), or when the kiln is bright red, for approximately 2 to 3 minutes. If you prefer, keep the kiln door open and remove the piece when you see the surface glossing over. The blue flux should look a whitish-blue after firing.

6

6 Flatten the cloisonné wire and then bend it to fit the picture exactly. Place the wires in position with a pair of stainless steel tweezers and using a dab of colourless enamelling glue if necessary. I used a mixture of gold and silver 0.3mm cloisonné wire, which I flattened through the rolling mill. Try to avoid using straight lines because cloisonné wire falls over easily.

7 When all the cloisonné wires are in place, refire the piece. The wires will just sink into the flux. Any still standing proud after firing can be gently pushed down with the burnisher when the piece has cooled.

8 Now fill in the colours. Work one at a time, taking care not to spill one over into another.

16 Finish the silver by polishing or leaving a satin finish.

17 Drill holes at the two top corners and loop through a jump ring, which is attached to the chain.

18 Using easy solder and taking care not to let the flame stray onto the enamel, solder the jump rings in place. I usually place the enamel upside down on the soldering block and cover it with a sheet of mica before soldering on jump rings.

19 If you do not wish to enamel the piece, and would like to oxidise the background formed after either etching the picture or forming it with wires, immerse the piece in a hot solution of potassium sulphide and simply polish away the oxide from the higher areas.

9 Fire at the temperature your test showed to be most suitable. It will probably be similar to the flux firing, and take a similar length of time, but keep checking to see when the enamels flow.

10 Remove the piece from the kiln and wait until it is cool before putting in the next layer of enamel. Continue firing, cooling and putting in more enamel until you have built up to a level just higher than the surrounding silver.

11 Under *running* water, rub a carborundum stone over your piece until the enamel is level and all the cloisonné wires are exposed.

12 Dry, and refill any low areas with enamel. Refire.

13 Rub down again under running water, this time working down through the wet and dry papers from numbers 280 to 600.

14 Fire again. This last firing should be slightly hotter and quicker than previous firings.

15 After this last firing the silver will probably have oxidized. It is usually safe to immerse the piece in a pickle of sulphuric acid. (Your test will have

told you if any of the enamels are unsuitable.) If you cannot pickle it carefully, remove the oxides with 600 wet and dry papers, taking care not to touch the enamel.

Technical Information

ANNEALING TEMPERATURES

	°F	°C
Copper	700–1200	370–650
Brass	800–1380	430–750
Gold (not 24 carat)	1200–1380	650–750
Silver	1120–1300	600–700

MELTING TEMPERATURES

	°F	°C
Copper	1980	1080
Brass	1660	900
Gold (not 24 carat)	1600–1830	880–1000
Silver	1640	890

SOLDER MELTING TEMPERATURES

	Hard		Medium			Easy
	°C	°F	°C	°F	°C	°F
9 carat Gold	755–795	1390–1465	735–755	1355–1390	720–650	1330–1200
14 carat Gold	750–785	1380–1445	—	—	710–730	1310–1350
18 carat Gold	790–830	1455–1525	730–765	1350–1410	700–715	1290–1320
Silver	745–778	1375–1430	720–765	1330–1410	705–725	1300–1340

SPECIFIC GRAVITIES

	%	oz/in³	gm/mm³
Platinum	21.5	11.74	20.34
Copper	8.93		
Gold	19.36	10.00	17.33
Fine Silver	10.56	5.74	9.95
Sterling Silver	10.40	5.68	9.84
18 carat Gold	16.13	9.32	16.15
9 carat Gold	12.27	7.09	12.29
14 carat Gold	14.83	8.57	14.85
Water	1.00	0.58	1.00
Perspex	1.20	0.70	1.21

TO CALCULATE WEIGHT OF SILVER AND GOLD SHEET

Sheet $50 \times 100 \times 1mm$:

Weight = volume × density. For example, to find the weight of a:

Silver sheet: $50 \times 100 \times 1mm \times 9.84 = 49.2gm$
$2 \times 4 \times 0.39in \times 5.68 = 1.772oz$

Gold sheet (18 karat): $50 \times 100 \times 1mm \times 16.15 = 80.7gm$
$2 \times 4 \times 0.39in \times 9.32 = 2.907oz$

To estimate the cost of the silver or gold in a piece of jewellery you must first know, or estimate, the weight. Multiply the weight by the cost per gram or oz of the metal.

DIMENSIONS OF A CIRCLE

If your circle has a diameter of 10cm, the circumference can be calculated as follows:

	$2\pi r$[radius]	$\pi \times$ diameter
Fractions	$2 \times \frac{22}{7} \times 5 = 31.42$	$\frac{22}{7} \times 10 = 31.42$
Decimals	$2 \times 3.141 \times 5 = 31.41$	$3.141 \times 10 = 31.41$

The diameter of a circle is found by multiplying the known circumference by 0.31831.
The area of a circle is: diameter × itself × 0.7854.
For example, the area of a circle with a diameter of 14mm = $14 \times 14 \times 0.7854 = 153.93$ sq mm

The volume of a rod is: diameter × itself × 0.7854 × height. For example,
the volume of a rod with a diameter of 3cm and 10cm high = $3 \times 3 \times 0.7854 \times 10 = 70.68$ cu cm

BIRMINGHAM (SHAKESPEARE) METAL GAUGE

Gauge	mm	in
7	0.5	0.020
8	0.55	0.022
9	0.6	0.024
10	0.7	0.028
11	0.8	0.032
12	0.9	0.035
13	0.95	0.037
14	1.1	0.043
15	1.2	0.047
16	1.3	0.051
18	1.5	0.059
20	1.65	0.065
22	1.85	0.073
24	2.1	0.083
28	3.2	0.126

WEIGHTS

Troy ounces are used in weighing precious metals:
1 troy ounce = 31.104gm

Avoirdupois ounces are used in weighing base metals:
1 avoirdupois ounce = 28.35gm

CARAT WEIGHT USED FOR WEIGHING STONES

1 carat = ⅕ gram

Carats are divided into points:
1 carat = 100 points
½ carat = 0.50 points
¼ carat = 0.25 points

Glossary

Anneal: To soften metal by heating and cooling at the correct temperature. Soft metal is easier to work.

Anvil: Heavy metal stand with flat top and bottom with a round protruding nose. Used for shaping, flattening, hardening, etc.

Argotec: A white powder mixed to a paste with either methylated spirits or water and then painted onto silver prior to heating to avoid fire stain.

Arkansas Stone: An abrasive stone used for sharpening graving tools and fine points. Should be kept well oiled in use.

Barrel Polisher: Rubber barrel containing small stainless steel burnishers which polishes small chains and rounded pieces by a continuous revolving movement.

Bearer Wire: The metal ring inside the bezel which forms the "shelf" on which the stone sits.

Bevel: The slope on the edge of a metal surface.

Bezel: The part of a ring which encompasses and fastens the stone.

Binding Wire: Steel wire which ties and holds parts together for soldering.

Borax: A flux used for soldering. It is mixed to a paste with water and painted onto the areas to be soldered.

Burnisher: Highly polished stainless steel tool. Hand held and used to produce a shiny surface by rubbing on to metal.

Cabochon: A polished precious or semi-precious stone which is not cut into facets.

Casting: A means of making an object by pouring molten metal into a shaped space, usually by burning out a wax model of the object.

Charcoal Block: Used in soldering as a level surface. Can be scraped and shaped as necessary and reflects heat well.

Chasing: Pushing or punching a line onto the front of metal to form a design or a series of lines.

Chenier: Silver/gold tubing. Can have walls of different thickness for different uses, e.g. hinges, choker and joints.

Claw Setting: A setting for a faceted stone which uses wires or "claws" to hold the stone. It has an open back which allows the light to reflect off the stone.

Coping Saw: A hand saw used like a piercing saw for cutting wood, plastics, etc.

Cotter Pin: Used for holding pieces together whilst soldering. If passed through a hole the two ends can be bent over to keep the tension.

Culet: The bottom edge of a faceted stone.

Dividers: Metal implement with two fine points. A screw action spaces the distance at which the two points are kept apart.

Drawplate: A steel plate with graded holes that can be round, triangular, D-shape, square, oval or rectangular. Annealed wire is drawn through the plate until the desired size and shape are achieved.

Electroplating: Means of transferring a thin coat of metal by the use of an electric current.

Enamelling: Fusing glass to metal at high temperatures.

Engraving: Cutting lines into, or removing areas from, metal with a sharp graver.

Etching: The use of acid to eat away exposed metal.

Facet: A flat polished surface on a gem stone.

File: A steel rod or thick sheet with "teeth" of varying sizes. Used for filing away metal. One stroke of the file cuts the metal, the reverse stroke does not.

Findings: The means by which jewellery is secured – can be hooks, pins, butterfly catches, hinge joints.

Fire Stain: A blackish shadow which appears on silver, usually after polishing. It is the result of the copper in the silver mixing with the oxygen in the air during heating.

Flux: A medium used to prevent oxidization to allow solder to join the metal parts.

Forging: Shaping metal with hammers by pushing and compressing it to the desired shape.

Former: A steel shape used as a support whilst shaping and forming metal.

Fusing: Joining metal together by melting the surfaces.

Gimp: Tiny piece of chenier squeezed together to hold the ends of nylon, tiger tail or silk threads.

Girdle: The widest edge of a faceted stone.

Gold: A precious metal of bright yellow colour, well known for its ductility and malleability.

Granulation: Tiny silver/gold balls either soldered or fused to a metal surface for decoration.

Graver: Steel tool with sharpened, shaped point used for engraving.

Hallmark: Stamped marks on a piece of silver verifying the maker, the metal used, the office where it was assayed – or tested – and the year in which it was stamped.

Hyfin: A white polish used after Tripoli during the polishing process.

Investment: A fine plaster mixed with water, poured into a tube around a wax model before casting.

Jointing Tool: A hand tool used for holding chenier or rod, to help cut a straight line across it.

Lead Block: A malleable support for metal used in shaping.

Leather Pouch: Leather piece slung underneath the pin/workbench to catch filings.

Mallet: A wooden or rawhide hammer that is used like a hammer but does not mark the former or the metal unless the metal is very soft.

Mandrel: A tapered steel rod, hand held for taping rings into shape.

Mica: Heat-resistant transparent sheet on which pieces to be enamelled are placed.

Micrometer: Hand tool which accurately measures the thickness of wire, sheet metal, drills, etc.

Mill: Set of stainless steel rollers used for reducing the thickness of metal.

Nickel Silver: A metal often used for costume jewellery.

Nitric Acid: Colourless acid which goes slightly blue when added to water and is used for "bright dipping" silver and for etching.

Oxides: Black or shadowy areas that appear when some metals are heated in air. Can be removed by pickling.

Pave Setting: Settings where stones are set flush with the metal and usually very close to each other.

Pendant Motor: A motor with hand-held flexible drive shaft with a variety of different tools used for drilling, texturing, polishing, etc.

Pickle: A solution, usually sulphuric acid and water, used after soldering and annealing to remove residual flux and oxides.

Piercing: Cutting out metal with a jeweller's or "piercing" saw which has very fine blades.

Pin: Wood block attached to a jeweller's bench used as a support.

Pitch: Mixture of Burgundy or Swedish pitch, plaster of Paris (or pummice powder) and tallow, that supports work during chasing and repoussé.

Planishing: Finishing the surface of metal with a highly polished planishing hammer. Planishing removes or flattens previous hammering marks.

Potassium Sulphide (Liver of Sulphur): Dissolved in water and used to deliberately oxidize a piece.

Pumice: An abrasive powder mixed with water used after pickling to clean the metal.

Repoussé: Working a design into metal from the back.

Rivet: Method of joining – usually a small pin passing through two or more planes and spread over on both ends.

Rouge: A fine polish used after all other polishing has been completed. The powdered form is mixed with water and painted onto soldered joints to stop the solder flowing in further heating.

Sandbag: A round leather pouch filled with sand used for shaping and supporting metal.

Scriber: Small pencil-like tool made from steel with a fine point used for marking patterns on metal.

Shank: The body of a ring that fits round the finger.

Silver: Soft, white metallic element, very malleable.

Soldering: Joining one piece of metal to another by means of heat, flux and solder.

Sprue: Rod attached to castings which forms a channel to the piece for the molten metal to flow down – after casting is complete the sprue is cut away.

Stoning: Rubbing down enamels under water to a flat surface with a carborundum stone.

Sulphuric Acid: Colourless acid that becomes pale blue when in use – used as a pickle for precious metals.

Swaging: Making U-shape from a flat piece of metal by placing it in a U-shape block and hammering it in with a former.

Tempering: Heating up the working end of a steel tool to soften it after it has been hardened.

Texture: An uneven surface given to metal to enhance its appearance.

Torch: Used for soldering usually with a combination of gas and air.

Tripoli: A brown polish usually used first in the polishing process.

Tweezers: Brass: used after heating metal to place it into and remove it from the pickle. Insulated: tweezers with insulated handles used for holding and placing pieces during soldering. Stainless steel: used for fine jewellery work.

Ultrasonic: A cleaner which passes ultrasonic waves through the stainless steel container. It is used with an ammonia/detergent to clean off polish from metal.

Work Hardening: When metal has been hammered, bent or shaped until it becomes unmalleable. It should then be annealed.

Index

Italic page numbers refer to illustrations

A

Acacia *26*
acetate, design transfer 30, *30*
acetone 21, *21*
acid 10, 21, *21*, 35, 71
 see also chemicals
acrylics 49, *49*
African blackwood *25, 26*
amber *53*
annealing 8, 32, *32*, 109
 drawing down wire 36
 gold 94
 kiln 20
 quenching 32
 reannealing 32
 and springiness 38
 temperatures 108
anvil *14, 15*, 22, 64, 109
aquamarines *28*
argotec 21, *21*, 35, *35*, 109
Arkansas stone *14, 15*, 66, 109
avoirdupois ounce 108

B

barrel polisher 109
basse taille enamelling 74, *74*
beads 22, 49, *50*
 pegging 82–3, *82, 83*
 silver, project 101–3
 stringing 50
bearer wire 36, 51, 58, 109
Benny, Gerald *97*
bevel 109
bezel 51–3, 109
 gold 96
bezel rocker 53
binding wire 109
 contamination caused by 35
Birmingham metal gauge 108
blocking 65, *65*
bolt ring 45
borax *32*, 33, 109
bow drill *14*
box catch 45, 92, *92*
boxwood *26*, 48
bracelet clasps 45
brass 8
 melting temperature 108
bright dip 21
Brittania silver 22
brooches *50, 69, 89*
 brooch pins 38, *38*
 earrings and brooch set
 (project) 59–62
 fittings 45, 60, 61, 62
 reticulated *81*
Brown, Ruta *27, 81, 88*
burnisher *14, 15*, 43, *43*, 53, 109

C

cabochon stones 82, *82*, 109
carbon paper, design transfer 30,
 30

carnelians *55, 88*
casting 77–80, *88*, 109
 cire perdue 77, 79, *79*
 commercial 80, *80*
 cuttlefish moulds 77–8, *77, 78*
 drop 77, 78, *78*
 enamelled necklace (project)
 104–7
 lost-wax technique 80
 pock marks 80
 rubber mould injection 80, *80*
 sprue 79, 80
centrifugal casting machine 77,
 79, *79*
chains 37, *37*, 39, *39*, 65, *65*
 enamelled necklace (project)
 104–7
champlevé enamelling 73, *73*, 76
charcoal block *32*, 109
chasing 68–9, *68, 69*, 109
 hammer 16, *16*, 64
 tools 16, *16*, 68
chemicals 10, 17, *17*, 21, *21*, 35
chenier *36*, 83, *83*, 84, 109
 bending 101–2, *101, 102*
 collet 84, *84*
 drawing down 37, *37*
 hinges 91, *91*
 spring pins 92
 stone settings 83, *83*
Church, Nancy *49*
circle, calculation of dimensions
 51, 108
circumference, calculation 51,
 108
cire perdue 77, 79, *79*
clasps 45, *45*
claw settings 84–6, *85, 86*, 109
cleaning jewellery 18–19, *18*,
 110
cloisonné enamelling 72, 74, *74*,
 106–7
cold-cast enamelling 49
collets 84–6, *84, 85, 86*, 96
compass 16
coping saw 109
copper 8, 71, 108
corners, cutting *31*, 31
cotter pin 35, 109
crucible *14*, 15
crystals *53*
cufflinks 45, *45*
culet (faceted stones) 83, *83*, 109
cutters *14*, 15
cutting edges 66, *66*
cutting metal 31
cuttlefish moulds 77–8, *77, 78*

D

design 16, *16*, 24–8, 30, *30*
diamonds *96, 97*
dividers 16, *16*, 109
doming 47, *47*
 earrings and brooch set
 (project) 59–62
 hair ornament (project)

98–100
 textured domes 59–62
doming block *14*, 15, 47
drawing 16, *16*, 27
drawing down wire 36–7, *36, 37*
drawplate *14*, 15, 36, 109
drills *14*, 15, 16, 17
drop casting 77

E

earrings *43*, 44, *54, 55*, 61, 71, *73,
 74, 76*
 earrings and brooch set
 (project) 59–62
ebony 48
Eburah, Brian *50*
electroplating 109
embossing punch 68, *68*
emeralds *26*
emery stick *14, 15*, 42
enamelling 22, 72–6, 109, 110
 basse taille 74, *74*
 champlevé 73, *73*, 76
 cloisonné 72, 74, *74*, 106–7
 cold-cast 49
 enamelled necklace (project)
 104–7
 gold 96, *97*
 gold foil 96
 grisaille 75, *75*
 pliqué à jour 74, *74*
engraving 21, 66–7, *66, 67*, 109
epoxy resin 48
equipment *see* tools and
 equipment
etching 21, 70–1, *71*, 73, 96, 109
 enamelled necklace (project)
 104–7

F

faceted stones 82, *82*, 83, *83*, 109
fastenings 90, 92, *92*
fichu joint 45, *45*
files 13, *13, 14*, 15, 22, 40, *40*,
 109
filing 40, *40*
findings 44–5, *44, 45*, 109
 earrings 61
 enamelled pieces 76
 non-metal jewellery 50
finishing 42–3
fire stain 21, 35, *35*, 109
flatplate *14*, 15
fluorspar *53*
flux *32*, 33, 109
 gold 94
 pickling 35
forging 64–5, *64, 65*, 98–100, 109
 hair ornament (project)
 98–100
former 109
frit 72
fusing 81, 109

G

gimp 109

girdle (faceted stones) 83, *83*,
 109
glass 49, *49*
 enamelling *see* enamelling
gold 8, 22, *22*, 93–7, 108, 109
 beads 22
 coloured 8, *26*, 93, 94
 etching 71, 96
 filing 96
 fluxing 94
 plating *71*
granulation 109
graver 51, 66, 67, *67*, 109
 raising grains 87
grisaille enamelling 75, *75*
guaiacum *see lignum vitae*

H

hair ornament (project) 98–100
hallmarks 109
hammers 13, *13*, 16, *16*, 22
 ball-pein (ball-peen) 13, *13*, 68
 chasing 16, *16*, 64, 68
 forming 64
 jeweller's 16, *16*
 planishing 16, *16*, 41, *41*, 64
 raising 16, *16*, 64
hinge joint 22, 91, *91*
hyfin 42, 109

I

inlaid work *26*
investment 79, 109

J

jeweller's wax 21, 66, 67
jointing tool *14, 15*, 109
joints 91, *91*
 fichu 45, *45*
 hinge 22, 91, *91*
 jump ring 37, *37*, 90
 overlapping 90, *90*
 riveted 45, 46, *46*, 48, 110
 soldering *see* soldering
jump ring 37, *37*, 90

K

kiln 20, *20*
 enamelling 72, 75
Koppen, Alexandra *39, 90, 97*
Krinos, Daphne *43, 52*

L

labradorite *28*
Lanyon, Marcia *50*
lapis lazuli *89*, 101–3
 silver ring set with (project)
 56–8
lead block 47, 64, 109
lighter fuel 21, 42
lignum vitae 26, 48
liver of sulphur 110
lost-wax casting technique 80

M

McAnally, Pat *89*
McGrath, Jinks 48, *55, 73, 74, 76, 90, 96, 97*
mallet 13, *13*, 110
mandrel 13, *13*, 110
matt finish 21, 41
matting punch 68, *68*
measuring tools 16, *16*
melting temperatures 108
metals 12, 22
　see also individual metals
mica 74, 76, 110
micrometer 110
mill 19, *19*, 110
modelling, wax 77–80, *79*
　modelling pens 79
moonstones *55*
　earrings and brooch set
　　(project) 59–62
Morphy, Chris *68, 69*

N

napkin ring *22*
needle file 13, *13*
nickel silver 8, 110
nitric acid 21, *21*, 70–1, 110
nylon thread 50

O

opals *97*
oval settings, calculation of bezel
　length 52
overlapping joints 90, *90*
oxides and oxidization 21, 35,
　43, *43*, 62, 104, 110

P

painted enamels 75, *75*
painted jewellery *48, 49*
papier mâché 48, *48*
Park, Rowena *49*
pave settings 87, *87*, 110
Payne, Brett *55, 89*
pearls 101–3
　pegging 82–3, *82, 83*
　stringing 50
pegging pearls and beads 82–3,
　82, 83
pendant motor 20, *20*, 22, 41, *41*,
　42, 110
photo-etching 71
pickle 17, *17*, 21, 32, 35, *35*, 110
pickling 32, 33, 35, *35*, 95
piercing 31, 110
　saw 13, *13*
pins 13, *13*, 45, 110
pitch 41, 52, 66, 67, 68, 69, 110
pitch bowl 16, *16*
planishing 41, *41, 54*, 110
　hammer 16, *16*, 41, *41*, 64
　punch 68, *68*
plating 35
platinum
　specific gravity 108
pliers 13, *13, 14, 15*, 22, 35
pliqué à jour enamelling 74, *74*

polishing 20, 21, 42–3, *42, 43*
　polisher 19, *19*, 20, *20*
　ultrasonic cleaner 18–19, *18*,
　　110
potassium sulphide 21, *21*, 110
projects
　earrings and brooch set 59–62
　enamelled necklace 104–7
　hair ornament 98–100
　silver, gold and copper
　　necklace with beads and
　　wooden discs 101–3
　silver ring set with oval lapis
　　lazuli 56–8
protective clothing 21, 35
Pruden, Anton *64*
punches 14, 15, 16, *16*, 41, *41*,
　47, 68, *68*
　embossing 68, *68*
　hollow-faced 68, *68*
　linear (tracer) 68, *68*
　making 41, 68
　matting 68, *68*
　modelling 68, *68*
　planishing 68, *68*
　repoussé and chasing 68–9, *68*
　setting stones with 53

Q

quartz *81*
quenching 17, 32

R

raising hammer 16, *16*
repoussé 68–9, *68, 69*, 110
resins 49
reticulation 81, *81, 88*
riffler file 14, *15*
rings
　engraving inside 66
　interlocking engagement and
　　wedding *28*
　polishing 42, *43*
　silver ring set with oval lapis
　　lazuli (project) 56–8
riveting 45, 46, *46*, 48, 110
rolling mill 19, *19*, 110
rosewood 26, 48, *48*
rouge 42, 110

S

sandbag 14, *15*, 47, 110
sawing metal 31
saws 13, *13*, 31, 109
scorper 87, *87*
scriber (scribe) *14, 15*, 110
setter's wax 51, 52
shank 110
side cutters *14, 15*
silver 8, 110
　annealing *see* annealing
　buying 22
　forging 64–5, *64, 65*
　melting temperature 108
　oxidizing 21, 35, 43, ,*43*, 62,
　　104, 110
　plating 35

pure (fine) 22
　quenching 17, 33
　riveting 46, *46*
　rolling 19
　Standard 22
　Sterling 22
　tube and rod 22, *22*
　weight, calculation 108
snips *32*
soldering 8, 32, *32*, 33–5, *33, 34, 35*, 60, 61, 110
　equipment 17, *17, 32*, 35
　gold 95
specific gravities 94, 108
spitstick 67, *67, 87*
spring fitting 45
spring pin 92, *92*
sprue 79, 80, 110
stakes 20, *20*, 64–5, *64*
stones 21, 48, 82
　bezel 51–3
　cabochon 82, *82*, 109
　carat weight 108
　chenier or tube, settings in 83, *83*
　claw settings 84–6, *85, 86*, 109
　collets 84–6, *84, 85, 86*
　conical 53
　culet 83, *83*, 109
　earrings and brooch set
　　(project) 59–62
　faceted 51, 82, *82*, 83, *83*,
　　84–5, *84*, 109
　flush settings 83, *83*
　girdle 83, *83*, 109
　gold, setting in 96
　irregularly shaped 53
　mounts 82
　open-back settings 51
　pave settings 87, *87*, 110
　raising grains 87, *87*
　rub-over settings 51–3, *51, 52, 53*, 84–5, *84*, 86
　silver ring set with oval lapis
　　lazuli (project) 56–8
　table 83, *83*
　uncut 53, *53*
stoning 76, 110
suede stick *14, 15*, 42
sulphuric acid 21, *21*, 110
swage block *14, 15*, 47
swaging 110

T

table (faceted stones) 83, *83*
tanzanite 53
tempering 110
templates 16
texture 27, 41, *41, 42*, 68, 110
　design sources 24
tiger tail 50
tigerion *69*
titanium 50, *50*
tools and equipment 10, 12–21,
　22, *13, 14, 16*, 36
　casting 77–80
　chasing 68
　chemicals *see* chemicals
　doming 47

　enamelling 72
　engraving 66, *67*
　etching 70
　forging 64
　large equipment 18–20, *18, 19, 20*
　polishing 42
　regrinding and polishing tools
　　22
　repoussé 68
　soldering 17, *17, 32*, 35
　texturing 41, *41*
　transferring designs to metal
　　30, *30*
　see also individual tools
top cutter *14, 15*
topaz *53*
torch 110
tourmaline *53*
tracing paper 30, *30*
triblet 13, *13*, 39, 51, 52
Tripoli 42, 110
troy ounce 108
tube, stone settings 83, *83*
tumbler 20, *20*
Turner, Steve *48*
turquoises *88*
Turtill, Jenny *71, 78*

U

U sections 47, *47*
ultrasonic cleaning 18–19, *18*,
　110
Untracht, Oppi
　*Metal Techniques for
　　Craftsmen* 8

V

Vallis, Allan *55, 88*
vices 22
　bench 13, *13*, 15
　hand *14, 15*
　jeweller's 13, *13*
Vincent, Paul *48*

W

walnut *48*
water of Ayr stone 35
wet and dry paper 21, 40, 41, 42
wire 36–9, *55*
　bearer *36*, 51, 58, 109
　binding 109
　chenier *see* chenier
　drawing down 36–7, *36, 37*
　forging 65, *65*
　gold 22, *22*
　jump rings 37, *37*
　riveting 46, *46*
　rolling 19
　sections available *36*
　silver 22, *22*
　twisting together 38, *38*
wood *25, 26*, 48, 101–3
work bench or table 12, *12*
work hardening 110
workshop 10–22, *10*, 11, 35, 71
　tools and equipment *see* tools
　　and equipment